# TrueFaced

# ExperienceGuide

## TrueFaced

# ExperienceGuide

**For use with TrueFaced ExperienceDVD and the Revised Edition**

## Bill Thrall, Bruce McNicol, and John Lynch

Contributors: Mark Carver, Judy Gomoll, Steve Parolini

NAVPRESS®

BRINGING TRUTH TO LIFE

## OUR GUARANTEE TO YOU

We believe so strongly in the message of our books that we are making this quality guarantee to you. If for any reason you are disappointed with the content of this book, return the title page to us with your name and address and we will refund to you the list price of the book. To help us serve you better, please briefly describe why you were disappointed. Mail your refund request to: NavPress, P.O. Box 35002, Colorado Springs, CO 80935.

NavPress
P.O. Box 35001
Colorado Springs, Colorado 80935

The Navigators is an international Christian organization. Our mission is to reach, disciple, and equip people to know Christ and to make Him known through successive generations. We envision multitudes of diverse people in the United States and every other nation who have a passionate love for Christ, live a lifestyle of sharing Christ's love, and multiply spiritual laborers among those without Christ.

NavPress is the publishing ministry of The Navigators. NavPress publications help believers learn biblical truth and apply what they learn to their lives and ministries. Our mission is to stimulate spiritual formation among our readers.

ISBN 1-57683-678-9

Cover Design: David Carlson Design
Cover Images: Digital Vision and PhotoDisc
Creative Team: Dan Rich, Steve Parolini, Darla Hightower, Pat Miller

Some of the anecdotal illustrations in this book are true to life and are included with the permission of the persons involved. All other illustrations are composites of real situations, and any resemblance to people living or dead is coincidental.

Unless otherwise identified, all Scripture quotations in this publication are taken from THE MESSAGE (MSG). Copyright © 1993, 1994, 1995, 1996, 2000, 2001, 2002. Used by permission of NavPress Publishing Group.

Printed in the United States of America

1 2 3 4 5 6 7 8 9 10 / 08 07 06 05 04

FOR A FREE CATALOG OF
NAVPRESS BOOKS & BIBLE STUDIES,
CALL 1-800-366-7788 (USA)
OR 1-416-499-4615 (CANADA)

# Contents

# Introduction

‎═Welcome to one of the most profound journeys this life affords. We are about to embark on a glorious ride of profound discovery and a new way of seeing. It is not new truth, but for many of us, it will be a new experience. In astounding and unusual ways, God appears to be revealing to the body of Christ, in this season, the power, healing, and freedom of trust-triggered grace. Many of us have been walking for some time, with all our might and speed, down a road we think will gain us God's pleasure and favor. And we have grown weary of walking and discouraged in what we've found. Saddest of all, we have little confidence of God's pleasure or delight. This experience we are about to walk into will bring us to a crossroads where we get to actually choose again how we want to live this Christian life. The promises made in this experience guide are so full of hope and joy that you will be tempted to dismiss them as hyperbole. But they are backed by a God who waits for you to try them on. See you at the crossroads. . . .

This first week of your **TrueFaced Experience** you will view and briefly discuss a message by John Lynch to introduce the **TrueFaced** concepts. The outline for this session follows.

Week One: Hope

# Experiencing TrueFaced Together

## Before you begin:

### For the Group Leader

If you are the designated leader for this TrueFaced Experience, please follow these guidelines to ensure a positive experience for all participants.

1. You'll need a copy of the *TrueFaced Experience DVD* set for your group. This introductory session uses DVD #1.

2. You are a facilitator for this, not a teacher. Follow the instructions closely and fight any temptation to expand on the material provided. This is a place for experiential learning, *not* lecture.

3. Don't worry if some questions are left unanswered. Unanswered questions are part of the discovery process.

4. Close the session with prayer, and then remind participants of their homework assignments for the coming session.

# Hope

## Welcome

Take a moment to greet one another. If you traditionally enjoy snacks with your group, have at 'em. Use the opening moments as people congregate for a brief time of fellowship.

## Video Message

Gather in front of the TV/monitor and watch John Lynch's message to introduce the TrueFaced Experience. This is a 35-minute presentation and was recorded live. You'll find this message on DVD #1. It's called "The TrueFaced Message" in your DVD menu.

## Processing "The TrueFaced Message"

After viewing the DVD, take 5 to 7 minutes to discuss the following questions in your group. In the weeks that follow you'll be exploring each of the ideas presented in the DVD in greater detail, so don't dwell on the specifics here. Think about what you just viewed and answer:

- What did you hear?
- What hope did this message give you?

**Note:** After watching this video message, you may feel compelled to invite friends or family members to experience this TrueFaced journey with you. Please do (as long as this is permissible in your small group or church school structure). This can be a life-changing experience.

## Closing Prayer

After exploring the processing questions together, close in prayer and review the homework for next week's session (see below).

## Introducing the Tool

This week and each of the coming eight weeks we will provide you with one "take-home" tool you can use to go deeper with your TrueFaced experience. This week, take time to complete the "Truth-Telling Tool" on your own (go to page 14). This tool gives you an opportunity to actually *act* on the truths in *TrueFaced*. Character is formed as we *act on truth* that touches our hearts. Acting is how we know we are *trusting* the truth. After you have completed your part of the tool, share it with one or two trusted friends. (It's important that your friends read the corresponding chapter in *TrueFaced* so they can fully understand the process you are experiencing. Share your copy of *TrueFaced* or encourage them to buy a copy for themselves.)

## Before the Next Session

Read chapter 1, "Keeping Up Appearances" in your *TrueFaced* book. Then complete the "Experiencing TrueFaced on Your Own" section for Week Two in this Experience Guide (go to page 19). Pray throughout the week that your discoveries will positively impact all aspects of your everyday life.

# Truth-Telling Tool

**1.** More than anything else, the TrueFaced journey is about trusting God and others with who you really are. As you will experience, *trust* always helps us become truth-tellers instead of mask-wearers. Yet, many people have decided they will no longer trust because they believe they have been let down too many times. They have lost hope. And, "hope deferred makes the heart sick" (Proverbs 13:12, NIV).

If you have lost hope—like Moses, Job, David, John the Baptist, Peter, and other wonderful followers of God—write down what has caused you to lose hope or to become disappointed. What has caused you to become downhearted or to stop anticipating God's goodness in your life? These may be things such as:

- Losing a job or a promotion
- Losing your health, being diagnosed with a life-threatening illness
- Losing a family member or your best friend
- Having someone you trusted betray you
- Having to bury a dream that you had counted on for years
- Disappointing yourself or others—too many times

**2.** Look through the topics of the eight TrueFaced sessions below. Identify and circle the two or three that you most long to receive as you go through this TrueFaced journey.

1. Hope

2. Authenticity

3. Identity

4. Safety

5. Love

6. Freedom

7. Healing

8. Dreams

**3.** Share your list with God. Ask him be your Father for this journey. He wants to hear the desires of your heart. Trusting God is worth more to him (and to you) than *any* of the items on this list. God is not a genie, but he is a loving Father in charge of all outcomes in your life. Giving your list to him is an *act of trust*, especially if at this time you are downhearted or disillusioned.

Now share this list with your trusted friends.

# Welcome to Week Two of your TrueFaced Experience. There are three parts to this and each subsequent week in your TrueFaced Experience.

## Week Two: Authenticity

**The first part** of each week—Experiencing TrueFaced on Your Own—includes a number of specific questions based on the related content in the *TrueFaced* book. Take time to read the assigned book chapter and to go through each question on your own. Use the space provided in this Experience Guide to record your thoughts, concerns, questions, and insights.

**The second part**—Experiencing TrueFaced Together—is a group experience that expands on the concepts you explored on your own and makes them come alive through creative, focused, and field-tested activities. Meet with your group to go through these activities and plan on 30-40 minutes to complete them each week.

**The third part** is a tool you can take home and use to go deeper with the TrueFaced experience. (You've already seen the first of these.) Complete these during the week following the TrueFaced experience.

## Experiencing TrueFaced on Your Own

### Before you begin:

**1.** Read chapter 1, "Keeping Up Appearances" in your *TrueFaced* book. Take time to soak up all the stories and thoughts. This will be the basis for answering the following questions. You may want to review the "Did You Discover?" questions at the end of the chapter as well. To dig even further into the background for this chapter, look up the related Scripture passages referenced in the back of the *TrueFaced* book in the "Notes" section.

**2.** Get out a pen or pencil and respond to the questions that follow. Keep in mind this is your personal workbook for examining the truths in *TrueFaced*. It's okay to spill the truth onto these pages: they are "for your eyes only." Let this become a journal of your exploration of what it means to be TrueFaced.

# Authenticity

**1.** Which of these masks do you recognize from your "wardrobe"? Use the space below to describe a recent or typical time when you have worn one of these masks.

- ☐ "I'm happy" mask
- ☐ "I'm better than most" mask
- ☐ "I'm very together" mask
- ☐ "I'm a victim of others" mask
- ☑ "I don't care" mask
- ☐ "I am self-sufficient" mask
- ☐ "I'm very important" mask
- ☑ "I'm competent enough to not need love" mask
- ☐ "I'm the expert" mask
- ☐ "I am the theologically trained professional" mask
- ☑ "I'm not hurt" mask
- ☐ "I have the answers" mask
- ☑ "I am independent" mask
- ☐ "I am cool" mask
- ☐ [other masks]

**2.** And we live in a "family" sending this unspoken message: "I prefer that you be who I want you to be rather than who you are, if it's all the same to you." (*TrueFaced*, page 32)

*I always put up a strong front even when I'm unsure. My past is not always a good foundation.*

Sometimes we wear masks in order to please others. Think about your extended family, workplace, church, and circle of friends. Is there someone from whom you hide your "painful junk" so their image of you won't be shattered? Which of your masks do you wear for them?

What reaction do you fear if you removed that mask and revealed the real you?

*abject justification*

**3.** "I feel betrayed—betrayed by what I have been taught, betrayed by my own behavior, and betrayed by my community of faith. Everyone there seems to be 'doing just fine.' . . . And most of all, I feel betrayed by God himself." (*TrueFaced*, page 21)

Those in "The Land of Doing Just Fine" group often feel betrayed, but they believe they must never let anyone know. When you feel betrayed, it probably means that someone has violated your trust, been false or disloyal to you, led you astray or deceived you, or divulged something confidential about you. Choose one or more from this list and describe a time when you felt betrayed by:

- What you were taught
- Your own behavior
- Your community of faith
- God
- Other

When you felt betrayed, how did you respond or resolve to protect yourself?

*angry" explosive*

**4.** The authors describe those of us in the "Still Searching for the Next 'New' Technique" group as people who have "been putting bailing wire on the issues of our lives" (*TrueFaced*, page 21). Bailing wire purportedly fixes anything broken on a farm—at least for a while. For suburbanites, it's like putting duct tape on a leaking pipe to avoid calling a plumber. Consider this list of life issues common to most of us.

- Weaknesses - *defensive*
- Limitations - *lack of understanding*
- Needs - *love*
- Self-protection - *full armor*
- Unmet expectations - *ability*
- Imbalance between my character (who I'm supposed to be) and my capacity (what I'm supposed to be able to do)

Identify one "hidden" issue in your life from this list that you are holding together figuratively with bailing wire or duct tape:

How bad would this "leak" in your life have to become for you to seek outside help?

If that issue were to worsen today, who would you call for help? What would you say?

**5.** Like an undiagnosed disease quietly spreading poison throughout our bloodstream, the decision to hide or ignore our guilt and hurt leaves the *act of sin* unresolved. We may recognize we don't have the energy we used to have, but we blame this on something or someone else and fail to recognize and understand that an invisible, inner enemy drains our energy and joy. We may try to ignore it or stuff it away, but though it may lie dormant for a while, unresolved sin is always buried *alive*. (*TrueFaced*, page 24)

Our natural tendency is to silence the voice of our own guilt, or at least numb it so we don't feel its sting. But what if we listened to our guilt and actually paid attention to how it feels? According to the biblical writers, what does guilt feel like? Read these passages to help you.

- Ezra 9:6
- Psalm 32:3-5
- Psalm 38:4-9
- Psalm 40:12
- Psalm 51:1-6

Describe a time when you finally listened to your guilt and took steps to admit your sin to someone you hurt. How did you feel to have your sin resolved?

**6.** Sometimes when we have been hurt by someone else's sin, our response is not to fight back, but to flee. How do you typically respond when you are sinned against or hurt by someone else? (Do you fight, get angry, or hurt back? Do you flee, minimize, rationalize, or spiritualize the hurt away?)

Illustrate how you respond with a story from your experience.

**7.** Reread the sobering story about Sharon at the end of chapter 1. As you read, underline (and then summarize below) phrases that describe:

Sins committed against or by Sharon

Sharon's involuntary responses

Inevitable effects in Sharon's behavior or heart

**8.** When an act of sin remains unresolved, it causes a *nagging sense in the heart that doesn't go away.* Note that it's a "nagging" sense. We're in no way describing a morbid search to uncover some deep, hidden sin, or, as one friend calls it, "that elusive omission I think is keeping me from God's will." No, unresolved junk will remind us of itself on a regular basis. We'll never have to search for it. But like plaque, cholesterol, or unanswered e-mail, unresolved sin builds up. Eventually we have so much junk in our lives that we're convinced God can barely tolerate us. (*TrueFaced*, page 29)

How does unresolved sin keep us from maturing?

What does a "nagging sense" look like?

Who should we tell about our unresolved sin? Why? Who should we not tell? Why?

# Experiencing TrueFaced Together

## Before you begin:

**1.** Get together with your group. If you are a part of a large group (such as a church school class), your teacher or leader will facilitate the experience. If you're doing this in a small-group setting, anyone can lead the group by following the directions in this section.

**2.** Consider the following guidelines for making the most of your group experience:

- When you are directed to form a small group for an activity, select people you know at least a little. If you are placed in a pair or trio with people you don't know, take a couple minutes to introduce yourselves. This will give you a good starting place for today's experiential activity.
- Follow the directions carefully, particularly as they relate to discussion in your small group. These directions have been designed to provide safe boundaries so you can share appropriately with others.
- The skills, techniques, and truths you discover during this experience are applicable in many other areas of life. Practice what you learn outside of small-group time.
- Above all, don't be anxious about the experiential activities in this guide. They aren't scary, "stand up in front of the group and share your life" experiences. Each Experiencing TrueFaced Together activity has been field-tested and is designed to ease you into participation. That's not to say what you learn will be fluffy, surface-level stuff. The experiences can be life-changing. We'll lead you into the deeper stuff. But come prepared to invest yourself in the experience. It will be worth it.

## For the Group Leader

If you are the designated leader for this TrueFaced Experience, please follow these guidelines to ensure a positive experience for all participants.

**1.** Make sure everyone has the necessary materials before the session. Each person should have a copy of *TrueFaced* and a copy of the *TrueFaced Experience Guide*. You'll also need a copy of the *TrueFaced Experience DVD* set for your group. This session uses DVD #1.

**2.** Review the DVD contents for each session and know right where to go to play them. Test your DVD player setup to avoid technical glitches.

**3.** You are a facilitator for this, not a teacher. Follow the instructions closely and fight any temptation to expand on the material provided. This is a place for experiential learning, *not* lecture.

**4.** Don't worry if some questions are left unanswered. Unanswered questions are part of the discovery process.

**5.** Close the session with prayer, and then remind participants of their homework assignments for the coming session.

## Authenticity

### Welcome

Take a moment to greet one another. If you traditionally enjoy snacks with your group, have at 'em. Use the opening moments as people congregate for a brief time of fellowship.

### Video Introduction

Gather in front of the TV/monitor and watch the video introduction to this session. It's called "Week 2: Authenticity/Unmasking" in your DVD menu.

---

## About the DVD

We highly recommend you use the DVD for your TrueFaced Experience as it adds a significant dimension to the study. John Lynch is your DVD host and offers lots of good thoughts and compelling real-life stories that can help you in your journey. However, if you don't have access to the DVD, you can alternately have someone read aloud John's abbreviated introduction that follows.

**John Lynch:** I can't think of a better journey to be taking a bunch of friends on. This is a journey into an environment that will free us from mask wearing into a bright, intensely alive world of authenticity.

From as far back as I can remember I carried this thought of being famous. Behind that childhood self-importance was a deep conviction that if I was talented, popular, interesting, and competent enough people would love me more. As I neared graduation from college at Arizona State University, it became painfully evident that I had not prepared well for anything but, well, graduation. So, to hide away until I could figure out my future, I drove to Isla Vista, California, and found a position waiting tables in a Greek-Italian restaurant. I told my friends (who were safely far away) a different story—that I was doing standup comedy at a local nightclub (I wasn't). I formed that particular mask to avoid the pity of my friends.

What has since brought me home and is beginning to heal me is this thought: "*learning to trust God and others with me.*" That has changed me from a deceiving mask wearer to a fragile, but authentic, true-faced believer. In the exercise you're about to participate in, you will have the opportunity to learn a thing or two from these people around you. They are not perfect, but God has a beautiful way of speaking through other people and making them who you need them to be. But don't worry, you're not in this alone: God will be there with you every step of the way, protecting, revealing, healing, and releasing.

---

## Introducing the Experience

Today we're going to apply TrueFaced principles in an activity we call "Unmasking." This experience begins to crack our masks—the masks that keep us from knowing God intimately, from being loved by others, and from realizing God's dreams for us. This experience helps us sample the exhilaration of authenticity, the joy of living a TrueFaced life.

## For an Enjoyable Experience

In order to make this experience excellent and beneficial to all, consider the following guidelines for your small- and large-group time:

- Bring a mindset that says, "I am for the other person's best."
- Allow other group members to answer their questions. Do not interrupt.
- Allow other group members to "keep" their answers. Do not correct.
- Allow other group members to share their answers. Do not counsel. Listening to others talk about their experiences is a wonderful affirmation for them.
- Allow other group members to experience safety. Do not discuss their answers outside your group, unless they give you permission to do so.

## The "Unmasking" Experience

**1.** Begin by forming a small group with one or two partners. Groups of three work best. This experience should take approximately 30 minutes.

**2.** In your small group, have each person choose one of the questions in the "Unmasking Questions" section. Each small-group member may answer any question—you don't have to all answer the same question although it's certainly okay if you do.

**3.** Take turns in your group sharing your answer to the question you've chosen. As others in your small group are talking, listen intently. Ask yourself "What am I learning?" not "What can I teach the others?" Consider what clarifying questions you might ask once a group member is finished talking. Clarifying questions include: "What did you mean by . . . ," "How did that affect you . . . ," or "Did you say . . . " questions, but not "Why" questions. You might want to jot these down in the "Notes" space.

**4.** After answering your question, have the rest of the group members each ask one clarifying question.

**5.** Pray for each group member after all clarifying questions have been answered. Then if you still have time, have each group member choose another question to answer and follow the same instructions.

## Unmasking Questions

**1.** How are you affected by mask wearing in relationships?

**2.** What are the circumstances that cause you to wear masks?

**3.** How does your theology give you hope in dealing with unresolved life and sin issues?

**4.** In your family of origin, were you able to love and be loved? Why or why not?

**5.** You can invite others in your group to suggest a new question for you to answer. This can be risky, but very rewarding. You choose whether to answer it or one of the questions provided.

## Processing the "Unmasking" Experience

Form one large group and discuss the following question for no more than three minutes: *What did you just experience?* Allow time for everyone who so desires to respond. Stay focused on the processing question and use the guidelines outlined previously to facilitate a healthy discussion.

## Closing Video and Prayer

After exploring the processing question together, play the video segment called "Week 2: Authenticity/ Unmasking Recap" on your DVD menu. Following this, close in prayer and review the homework for next week's session.

## About the DVD

We highly recommend you use the DVD for your TrueFaced Experience as it adds a significant dimension to the study. However, if you don't have access to this DVD, you can alternately have someone read aloud the summary that follows.

**John Lynch:** This authenticity stuff can feel as awkward as the "ladies choice" skate at a junior high school mixer. You're calculating risk, reward, and considering opting out while the opting's good.

First, don't worry. We've all been there. We're mostly still there. Second, you're normal. But don't miss this: Where we are heading has health, freedom, and playful joy written all over it. Relax and take it slow. The only thing you need to pack for this trip is an open heart and a sincere motive.

And by the way, if you're asked to do assignments during this series, please do them. They're strategically designed to strengthen the experience. We've gone through exactly what you're being asked to try. And I can only say, you're in for one of those "sacred life gifts" God surprises us with from time to time.

Have a great week! See you next time.

## Before the Next Session

Read chapter 2, "To Please or to Trust?" in your *TrueFaced* book. Then complete the "Experiencing TrueFaced on Your Own" section for Week Three in this Experience Guide (go to page 37). Pray throughout the week that your discoveries will positively impact all aspects of your everyday life.

# Introducing the Tool

If you want to go deeper with your TrueFaced experience, take time in the coming week to complete the "Unmasking Tool" on your own. This tool gives you an opportunity to actually *act* on the truths in *TrueFaced*. Character is formed as we *act on truth* that touches our hearts. Acting is how we know we are *trusting* the truth. After you have completed your part of the exercise, share it with one or two trusted friends. (It's important that your friends read the corresponding chapter in *TrueFaced* so they can fully understand the process you are experiencing. Share your copy of *TrueFaced* or encourage them to buy a copy for themselves.)

## Unmasking Tool

**1.** Briefly write out how you have experienced the inevitable effects of sin in your life—both your sin and the sin of others toward you—in one or more areas below. (As you describe these behaviors you are preparing for an adventure that could transform your life.)

- Shame
- Blame
- Fear

- Anger
- Denial

**2.** Briefly write out how you have experienced one or more of these six masking behaviors listed in *TrueFaced*. Be specific.

- I become highly sensitized to my own sin and judge the sin of others.
- I lose my objectivity in a crisis and I become the issue.
- I hide my sinful behavior and become vulnerable to more sin.

- I am unable to be loved or to love.
- I become susceptible to wrong life choices.
- I attempt to control others.

**3.** Which of these masking behaviors will you trust God to remove in the next months and years? Which masks will you trust your close friends with? Meet with one friend to tell them about this masking behavior. Let your friend know how you are trusting them with this masking.

Welcome to life in The Room of Grace. Life here is sometimes messy and not always easy, but it can be profoundly healing and maturing.

# Week Three: Identity

# Experiencing TrueFaced on Your Own

## Before you begin:

**1.** Read chapter 2, "To Please or to Trust?" in your *TrueFaced* book. Take time to soak up all the stories and thoughts. This will be the basis for answering the following questions. You may want to review the "Did You Discover?" questions at the end of the chapter as well. To dig even further into the background for this chapter, look up the related Scripture passages referenced in the back of the *TrueFaced* book in the "Notes" section.

**2.** Get out a pen or pencil and respond to the questions that follow. Keep in mind this is your personal workbook for examining the truths in *TrueFaced*. It's okay to spill the truth onto these pages: they are "for your eyes only." Let this become a journal of your exploration of what it means to be TrueFaced.

# Identity

1. A motive is an inner drive or desire that causes a person to act in a certain way. A motive produces values that, in turn, produce multiple actions:

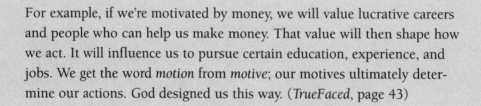

Motive → Values → Actions

For example, if we're motivated by money, we will value lucrative careers and people who can help us make money. That value will then shape how we act. It will influence us to pursue certain education, experience, and jobs. We get the word *motion* from *motive*; our motives ultimately determine our actions. God designed us this way. (*TrueFaced*, page 43)

Let's begin by exploring our motives, those inner desires that drive major choices in our lives and shape how we choose to live (where, with whom, doing what). Reflect, first, on some early motives in your life.

a. What was your inner desire as you were growing up?

b. What things did you enjoy and value?

c. How did your choices reflect your motive and values?

d. As you entered adulthood, identify your:

■ Basic Motive ("What I believed was true . . . "):

_____

■ Basic Values ("It was important to me that . . . "):

_____

■ Important Actions ("So I decided to . . . "):

_____

**2.** Yet, as weeks turn into months, I can't help noticing that many people in this room sound a bit cynical and look pretty tired. Many of them seem alone. . . . Quite a few seem superficial—guarded. [A little mask-wearing, maybe?] . . . I no longer feel as comfortable or relaxed here. I have this nagging anxiety that if I don't keep behaving well—if I don't control my sin enough—I'll be on the outs with everyone in the room. And with God! . . . But the more time I spend in The Room of Good Intentions, the more disappointment I feel. Despite all my striving, all my efforts, I keep sinning! In fact, some days I'm fixated simply on trying *not* to sin. I seem to never be able to get around to doing things to please God. It takes all my energy to avoid doing those things that *displease* him! Other days I can't seem to do enough. I never get through my list of things to work on. It feels like I am making every effort to please a God who never seems pleased enough! (*TrueFaced*, pages 39-40)

If we spend enough time in The Room of Good Intentions, we begin to notice some troubling and unsatisfying effects. In the excerpt above, circle the troubling behaviors you find among those of us whose motive is a determination to please God with our efforts.

How many of those troubling behaviors describe your home, church, ministry, or workplace? (Be as objective as possible when you answer this question.)

**3.** As do all of us, Adam and Eve's two sons had to choose what to do with their guilt and hurt. The authors state that Cain "chose the path of Pleasing God and paid dearly for it" (*TrueFaced*, page 46). Although the details of the story are sketchy, Scripture tells us that:

> Cain brought an offering to God from the produce of his farm. Abel also brought an offering, but from the firstborn animals of his herd, choice cuts of meat. God liked Abel and his offering, but Cain and his offering didn't get his approval. Cain lost his temper and went into a sulk. (Genesis 4:3-5, MSG)

The writer to the Hebrews teaches that Abel chose the path of Trusting God:

By an act of faith, Abel brought a better sacrifice to God than Cain. It was what he **believed**, not what he **brought**, that made the difference. That's what God noticed and approved as righteous. After all these centuries, that belief continues to catch our notice . . . [because] **it's impossible to please God apart from faith.** (Hebrews 11:4,6, MSG, emphasis added)

Why do you think Abel's choice represented an act of faith, but Cain's didn't? (Hint: What do you think the two brothers believed?)

Cain became so angry that he ended up killing his younger brother Abel. As you read his conversation with God after his act of sin, note and under-line any traces of the involuntary responses (guilt and hurt) and of the inevitable effects (anger, denial, shame, blame, and fear) that you can find. Write some of your thoughts in the space below.

What does trusting God have to do with what we "give" to him?

**4.** Having explored the house at the end of the road marked Pleasing God, let's consider the less traveled road of Trusting God. This road represents a radically different way to deal with our guilt and hurt—a way that first invites and then requires us to discard our masks. To get a picture of it, refer to pages 40-43 in *TrueFaced*, and fill in the blanks below.

- Road (given): ___ Trusting God ___
- Room (given): ___ Room of Grace ___

▪ High Value: _____

▪ Enter by: _____

▪ Actions: _____

According to those in The Room of Grace, what is the goal of living the way of trust? What advice do you believe people in The Room of Grace would give you on how to reach that goal? Complete the following chart with this in mind:

| Verse | Goal (Trusting God for what?) | Means (How to reach the goal) |
|-------|-------------------------------|-------------------------------|
| Matthew 28:20 | To obey Jesus in everything he commands. | |
| Acts 18:9-10 | To have strength to speak for Jesus in hostile arenas. | |
| Romans 5:6-8 | To be rescued, to avoid death. | |
| Hebrews 13:5 | To be content, not greedy. | |

What is your response to this perspective on how the goal will be reached?

**5.** The two paths appear in the same verse in Hebrews 11:6. Did you notice that trusting God (having faith in God) is what really pleases him most? In fact, without trusting God it is absolutely impossible to please him, no matter how hard you work at it!

Think of a time when someone said to you, "Just trust me, Honey!" How do you respond to "just trusting"? Why?

As a parent, which would you prefer from your child?

- That he or she diligently strives to please you and earn your approval all the time
- That he or she relaxes in unquestioning assurance of your love and trusts your guidance

As you reflect on your life, what significant event or experience stands out to you as a moment when God was saying (whether or not you heard him at the time), "Trust me"? What was the specific issue he was addressing? What were the long-term results of your choice?

**6.** After exploring the two fundamental motives (Pleasing versus Trusting), let's explore the value that flows out of trusting God: Living Out of Who God Says I Am. When God redeemed you at the infinitely costly price of his Son, he gave you a new identity. Now he says you're his beloved child!
Complete the chart below describing what is true about you now, according to this new identity:

| Verse | What is true about me | Verse | What is true about me |
|---|---|---|---|
| Ephesians 1:3 | | Ephesians 2:13 | |
| Ephesians 1:4 | | Ephesians 3:6 | |
| Ephesians 1:5 | | Ephesians 3:17-19 | |
| Ephesians 1:7 | | Ephesians 5:29 | |
| Ephesians 1:7-8 | | Isaiah 43:4 | |

According to these passages, is your identity a current, ongoing reality *because* you trust God, or a future reality *if* your behavior pleases God enough? Explain.

If you are not trusting in God to bring you to maturity, who or what else are you trusting to get the job done? What difference would it make which identity you live out of?

**7.** Of course, many people talk as if they have taken the Trusting God road, but in reality they live in The Room of Good Intentions. Why do so many people say the right thing, but then live the wrong life? We call this sweeping reality in the church today The Great Disconnect. . . . A missionary executive couple, a seasoned counselor, professional teachers and retreat speakers. Each projected a marriage, a life, and a ministry that was "together," healthy. Each can quote Scripture on demand, teach excellent Bible lessons, and instruct others about what it means to be "in Christ." Together they influence thousands who look to them for spiritual direction. Yet, their masked reality tells a very different story about what they really believe about themselves and their circumstances. Taking the road marked Pleasing God, many, many Christians never understand or live out what it means to be "in Christ Jesus." (*TrueFaced*, pages 49-50)

Review the three stories on pages 49-50 of *TrueFaced* about Christians who claimed to trust God, but whose lives were very disconnected from who they pretended to be. Choose the story that touches you the most. Describe below the tension you experience in this disconnect.

How can people live their life disconnected from the truths they say they believe and attempt to teach to others?

**8.** A hesitancy to trust God almost always goes along with a hesitancy to trust people. "Just trust me!" is the last thing you want to hear when you have already carefully concluded that no one can be trusted . . . except yourself. You find yourself thinking,

> "I'll nurture a relationship of trust, all right, just with myself. Sorry, I can't go down that trust road anymore. Nice sounding, I'll give you that. But way too much pain, too much risk, too many unmet expectations with the faces of those who failed me brightly etched in my memory. You might have almost convinced me when I was in my teens, but not now. Way too much data standing in the way of believing that pipe dream. Nope. Ain't going there. I may fail, but it will be me failing. And I'll have no one to blame but me. I like it that way. I take the blame, I get the credit. I will be the master of my fate, the captain of my soul. Me, I can trust. God, maybe. Even he does some weird stuff I can't figure out. But trusting others with me, my dreams, my cherished hopes, you gotta be kidding! I may look like I just fell off the turnip truck, but that's only because I'm bruised from the beating I took trusting others." (from *Beyond Your Best,* Thrall, et. al, page 40)

Has there been a time in your life when you consciously decided that it was too risky to trust others and that you would just have to trust yourself? Describe that time and what happened as a result of your decision to trust yourself.

**9.** If we refuse to enter The Room of Grace, we will constantly be striving in The Room of Good Intentions. We will strive to change into something we are not yet: godly. In The Room of Grace we grow up and mature into something that is already true about us: godly. The first room creates a works-based, performance-driven relationship with God and puts the responsibility on our resources. The second room places the responsibility on the resources of God. God is not interested in changing you. He already has. The new DNA is set. God wants you to believe that he has already changed you so that he can get on with the process of maturing you into who you already are. Trust opens the way for this process—for God to bring you to maturity. If you do not trust God, you can't mature, because your focus is messed up. You're still trying to change enough to be labeled godly. (*TrueFaced*, page 53)

In your opinion, what's the difference between striving to change ourselves and maturing?  *allowing God to work through me.*

Answer this question: Does the God who lavishly provides you with his own presence, his Holy Spirit, working things in your lives you could never do for yourselves, does he do these things because of your strenuous moral striving or because you trust him to do them in you? (Galatians 3:5, MSG)

According to this passage, why is it foolish for you to strive to change into being godly? What is God interested in?

**10.** In closing this study, let's eavesdrop on the conversation between John (the young, gifted preacher) and Bill (his boss and mentor).

> **John:** I think there are about two or three issues that I haven't yet overcome. They're not too complex or difficult. Once they get solved I really think I can be used by God in a big way.
>
> **Bill (Response 1):** Well, let's get to work on those. What are they? Let's look at them one at a time and solve them so you can really take off.
>
> **Bill (Response 2):** John, then I hope that you never, ever completely solve those issues. You will become self-dependent. You will become self-sufficient. The goal is not for you to get all of your "stuff" solved. You never will. There is an endless list of stuff. God is gracious to reveal only a snippet at a time. The goal is to learn to depend on—to trust—what God says is true about you, so that together you can begin dealing with that stuff. (*TrueFaced*, page 55)

Which of these two "roads" represents the road less traveled by? Why do you think it has meant all the difference in John's maturing?

If we are not called to deal with our "stuff" by striving to change ourselves for the better, then how are we to deal with it?

Is there some shattered dream of yours that you want to bring to Jesus now? A wounded heart, a broken toy? You can do so in prayer. Relax, and trust him with you . . . with your pain.

# Experiencing TrueFaced Together

## Before you begin:

**1.** Get together with your group. If you are a part of a large group (such as a church school class), your teacher or leader will facilitate the experience. If you're doing this in a small-group setting, anyone can lead the group by following the directions in this section.

**2.** Consider the following guidelines for making the most of your group experience:

- When you are directed to form a small group for an activity, select people you know at least a little. If you are placed in a pair or trio with people you don't know, take a couple minutes to introduce yourselves. This will give you a good starting place for today's experiential activity.
- Follow the directions carefully, particularly as they relate to discussion in your small group. These directions have been designed to provide safe boundaries so you can share appropriately with others.
- The skills, techniques, and truths you discover during this experience are applicable in many other areas of life. Practice what you learn outside of small-group time.
- Above all, don't be anxious about the experiential activities in this guide. They aren't scary, "stand up in front of the group and share your life" experiences. Each Experiencing TrueFaced Together activity has been field-tested and is designed to ease you into participation. That's not to say what you learn will be fluffy, surface-level stuff. The experiences can be life-changing. We'll lead you into the deeper stuff. But come prepared to invest yourself in the experience. It will be worth it.

## For the Group Leader

If you are the designated leader for this TrueFaced Experience, please follow these guidelines to ensure a positive experience for all participants.

**1.** Make sure everyone has the necessary materials before the session. Each person should have a copy of *TrueFaced* and a copy of the *TrueFaced Experience Guide*. You'll also need a copy of the *TrueFaced Experience DVD* set for your group. This session uses DVD #1.

**2.** Review the DVD contents for each session and know right where to go to play them. Test your DVD player setup to avoid technical glitches.

**3.** You are a facilitator for this, not a teacher. Follow the instructions closely and fight any temptation to expand on the material provided. This is a place for experiential learning, *not* lecture.

**4.** Don't worry if some questions are left unanswered. Unanswered questions are part of the discovery process.

**5.** Close the session with prayer, and then remind participants of their homework assignments for the coming session.

# Identity

## Welcome

Take a moment to greet one another. If you traditionally enjoy snacks with your group, have at 'em. Use the opening moments as people congregate for a brief time of fellowship.

## Video Introduction

Gather in front of the TV/monitor and watch the video introduction to this session. It's called "Week 3: Identity/ Connecting" in your DVD menu.

## Introducing the Experience

Today we're going to apply TrueFaced principles in an activity we call "Connecting." This experience connects two things that most of us have a hard time joining: What I *say* is true about me with how I actually *live*. We call this kind of fragmented living — saying one thing is true but living as if another thing is true — The Great Disconnect. This activity will help you experience The Great Connect as you enter the The Room of Grace.

## For an Enjoyable Experience

In order to make this experience excellent and beneficial to all, consider the

---

## About the DVD

We highly recommend you use the DVD for your TrueFaced Experience as it adds a significant dimension to the study. John Lynch is your DVD host and offers lots of good thoughts and compelling real-life stories that can help you in your journey. However, if you don't have access to the DVD, you can alternately have someone read aloud John's abbreviated introduction that follows.

**John Lynch:** We've presented to you a compelling visual metaphor of two ways to live this Christian life: The Room of Good Intentions and The Room of Grace. The rooms are pretty much mutually exclusive. They emanate from two well-defined *heart motives* in how we relate to God: Pleasing God or Trusting God. And, like it or not, we are presently living in one these two rooms.

Many of us, as we examine our lives in The Room of Good Intentions, feel foolish. "How did my life get here? I didn't sign up with Jesus for this kind of hollow, inauthentic, religious experience of low-grade guilt and anxiety! What happened?" *Actions* happened. Predictable actions from distorted values created out of motives revealed by unresolved sin. The Room of Good Intentions didn't just happen to us. And getting out of this room won't just happen either. Our motives must change. Then the insanity of doing the same thing over and over and expecting different results, it too will change.

The experiential activity for today's session is designed to help us discover what we think we are gaining by staying in The Room of Good Intentions. It will also give us a pretty good read on what we gain living in The Room of Grace.

following guidelines for your small- and large-group time:

- Allow other group members to answer their questions. Do not interrupt.
- Allow other group members to "keep" their answers. Do not correct. This is a *discovery* process, not a declaration of fact. No one should have to defend any answer.
- Allow the other group members to experience safety. Do not discuss their answers outside your group, unless they give you permission to do so.

## The "Connecting" Experience

**1.** Begin by forming a small group with one or two partners. Groups of three work best. This experience should take approximately 30 minutes.

**2.** On your own, think about and write answers to the "Connecting Questions" in the section.

**3.** After everyone's finished writing, take turns sharing your answers with your small group. Allow no more than five minutes per group member for this sharing time.

**4.** When everyone has shared, pray for one another to practice "connecting" each time this month you encounter an opportunity to live out of who God says you are.

### Connecting Questions

**1.** When you are struggling with "believing" what God says is true about you, what causes you to stay trapped in The Room of Good Intentions and what frees you into The Room of Grace? Which room takes sin most seriously? Explain your answer.

**2.** When you have tried to get out of The Room of Good Intentions, did others try to stop you? What was that like? How did that make you feel? (Please don't mention names.)

**3.** What does it cost you to connect what God says is true about you with how you actually live? How do you do that?

**4.** You can invite others in your group to suggest a new question for you to answer. This can be risky, but very rewarding. You choose whether to answer it or one of the questions provided above.

Notes:

## Processing the "Connecting" Experience

Form one large group and discuss the following question for no more than three minutes: *What did you just experience?* Allow time for everyone who so desires to respond. Stay focused on the processing question and use the guidelines outlined previously to facilitate a healthy discussion.

## Closing Video and Prayer

After exploring the processing question together, play the video segment called "Week Three: Identity/ Connecting Recap" on your DVD menu. Following this, close in prayer and review the homework for next week's session (see below).

## Before the Next Session

Read chapter 3, "Grace Works!" in your *TrueFaced* book. Then complete the "Experiencing TrueFaced on Your Own" section for Week Four that follows. Pray throughout the week that your discoveries will positively impact all aspects of your everyday life.

## About the DVD

You will need the *TrueFaced Experience DVD* for the small group portion of your TrueFaced Experience. If you don't have the DVD, you can substitute the following abbreviated conclusion to the small group experience.

**John Lynch:** What we experience together in relationships of growing trust is a process that helps us examine the consequences of our choice to live either in The Room of Good Intentions or in The Room of Grace. This can be a very revealing process, for it helps us discover where we believe we really are in relationship with God. By the time we finish, we hope to be able to describe which room we feel most connected to in real time. Not which one we wish we connected with, but which room we actually find ourselves in.

Don't dance around this. All growth begins with a vulnerable humility that stops us from lamenting where we *should* be and allows God to show us where we really *are*, so he can take us where he wants us to be.

Take care of each other as God takes care of you!

# Introducing the Tool

If you want to go deeper with your TrueFaced experience, take time in the coming week to complete the "Connecting Tool" on your own. This tool gives you an opportunity to actually *act* on the truths in *TrueFaced.* Character is formed as we *act on truth* that touches our hearts. Acting is how we know we are *trusting* the truth. After you have completed your part of the exercise, share it with one or two trusted friends. (It's important that your friends read the corresponding chapter in *TrueFaced* so they can fully understand the process you are experiencing. Share your copy of *TrueFaced* or encourage them to buy a copy for themselves.)

## Connecting Tool

**1.** Which unresolved sin issue breaks your intimacy with God most often or most deeply? How has working strenuously on that sin issue to achieve an intimate relationship with God left you frustrated, defeated, or even despairing?

**2.** According to the biblical truth expressed in *TrueFaced*, what is God's answer of hope for you? Will you commit to this answer?

Which of the following most threaten to move you away from that answer of hope for this unresolved sin: your theology, your key relationships, or your commitments to a leader or others in The Room of Good Intentions?

**3.** Share with a trusted friend your commitment to stay on the path and in the room that leads to actually *living* out this maturing answer of hope. Ask for their prayer and their encouragement. (Note: It is possible for any of us to be in The Room of Grace with one issue in our lives and, at the same time, also choose The Room of Good Intentions for another issue! Such is the nature of growing in trusting God and others with us.)

# Week Four: Safety

# Experiencing TrueFaced on Your Own

## Before you begin:

**1.** Read chapter 3, "Grace Works!" in your *TrueFaced* book. Take time to soak up all the stories and thoughts. This will be the basis for answering the following questions. You may want to review the "Did You Discover?" questions at the end of the chapter as well. To dig even further into the background for this chapter, look up the related Scripture passages referenced in the back of the *TrueFaced* book in the "Notes" section.

**2.** Get out a pen or pencil and respond to the questions that follow. Keep in mind this is your personal workbook for examining the truths in *TrueFaced*. It's okay to spill the truth onto these pages: they are "for your eyes only." Let this become a journal of your exploration of what it means to be TrueFaced.

## Safety

**1.** Describe a time when someone else's humility brought out compassion and grace in you or a time when someone else's pride rebuffed your grace.

**2.** This chapter opens with a story about Mark, a gifted analyst/problem-solver who had explored both paths of Striving and Trusting.

Reread Mark's story in *TrueFaced* once, circling the words *believe* and *trust* whenever you see them. What Mark believed to be true about himself, what he trusted or didn't trust, profoundly influenced the efforts and actions he took as well as the inevitable effects on his heart.

Study the story one more time, filling in the chart below as you go.

| Mark in The Room of Good Intentions | | Mark in The Room of Grace | |
|---|---|---|---|
| **What he believed/trusted (especially about himself)** | **His actions/efforts** | **What he believed/trusted (especially about himself)** | **His actions/efforts** |
| (example) Mother didn't love me | (example) Tried anything & everything | (example) I am who God says I am | (example) Untruths, sin issues, striving slid off me |
| | | | |

Mark says that in The Room of Grace he got in touch with the same gift of trust that God gave him when he came to know Jesus. Pause as you begin this study to do the same. Revisit that "gift of trust" that you received when you came to know Jesus. In what ways were you most challenged to *trust* as you took those initial steps of faith? Share your story with someone this week.

**3.** When we turn the knob of Humility, we walk right into The Room of Grace. Like a mutual friend introducing us to our future spouse, humility escorts us to grace. Humility requires trust. It is her core feature. Humility believes that I can trust God to teach, direct, and protect me. Humility also believes that God has provided others in my life to do the same. In this case, I am depending on God to tell me how the world looks and works, giving up my rights to notions I had before. I am "leaning into" his evaluation of reality, one I did not previously have or know. This is why we define humility as *trusting God and others with me*. (*TrueFaced*, page 62)

From this quote, what are several things you discover about humility?

**4.** Grace can never be earned, but it can be spurned through untrust, the absence of humility. We never deserve grace—it is always unmerited—but we can invite grace into our lives, we can attract it. How? By trusting God. God gives his grace to those who trust him—to the humble. (*TrueFaced*, page 62)

Read 1 Peter 5:5-7 in your Bible, as well as from *The Message* below:

And you who are younger must follow your leaders. But all of you, leaders
and followers alike, are to be down to earth with each other, for—

God has had it with the proud,
But takes delight in just plain people.

So be content with who you are, and don't put on airs. God's strong hand
is on you; he'll promote you at the right time. Live carefree before God;
he is most careful with you.

What part does humbling yourself play in eventually reaching the place
God has for you?

What are the results if you depend pridefully on your own efforts and opinions?

**5.** "O, God, I am lower than sludge clinging to a rock in the deepest part of
the sea, which receiving no light, causes all near to wonder if it exists at all.
I am and shall remain the pitiful chorus of a hollow dirge, fit only for the
recounting of what might have been." (*TrueFaced*, page 62)

OK, OK. So this is a bit exaggerated. Nevertheless . . . is this an expression
of humility or of pride? Explain.

You've probably never thought of yourself as "lower than sludge clinging to a rock." But in your deeper periods of dissatisfaction with yourself, what *have* you told yourself about you? Record a typical inner tape from those periods of your life. Perhaps begin with "Oh, God, I am not . . . "

In what way might your words reflect pride instead of humility?

Summarize the most important things you have learned so far from *TrueFaced* about pride and humility, especially as they relate to trust and grace.

| Pride | Humility |
| --- | --- |
| (example) Shuts grace down | (example) Attracts God's grace to me |
| | |

**6.** False humility is just one species of pride, and it creates an unhealthy portrait of who I am. And how I see myself deeply influences my identity. So when grace paints a portrait of me, what does it look like?

In this life, we who have trusted Christ will always have sin issues, and we will always have the identity God gave us. They are constants. Unchanging realities. (*TrueFaced*, page 64)

Working on My Sin Issues ———————————————————⟶

Trusting Who God Says I Am ———————————————————⟶

It's key that we ask ourselves: Which one of these two constants defines my life focus? Which offers me the hope of experiencing the other? If we opt for the top line, we will never experience the bottom line. But, if we focus on the bottom line, we will experience unparalleled transformation regarding our sin issues. It's a whole new way of seeing. (*TrueFaced*, page 64)

Remember John (from the last chapter) who planned to work on the two or three issues that he hadn't yet overcome, expecting that effort to clear him for takeoff so he could then be used by God in a big way? Bill helped him accept that he will always have sin issues—if not the old ones, then some new ones along the way. But he should never allow his sin issues to define his identity or kidnap his life focus. Is your view of yourself more like John's or Bill's? Which of the constants is dominating your life focus (and therefore your identity) right now? Explain.

**7.** Many Christians know God loves us and wants to be with us, but we also believe our sin has put an impossible mass between God and us. We understand that Jesus has made a way for us to one day be together in heaven, but right now—until we get better, do better, or start to take things seriously—we believe we'll have to settle for rare moments of intimacy with him. We know ourselves too well, and there is no way we're ever going to be able to keep from sinning. We believe God loves us, but we also believe he's pretty disappointed with us. We expect to see him someday, but for now we can only hope that some days we will feel his touch on our lives. That's as good as it gets on this earth . . . or so we've come to believe. (*TrueFaced*, page 65)

Do you feel that God is disappointed with you somehow? Explain.

Reread the description of the imaginary lake found on pages 65-66 in *TrueFaced*.

How does that "lake" describe your present realities?

How do those realities affect your hope—your discouragement?

**8.**

| Grace as a Theology to Believe | Grace as an Environment to Enjoy |
|---|---|
| Many of us understand grace as a theological position. And it is delightfully that. Undeserved, unending, unearned, unwavering, grace is God's inexhaustible love and absolute acceptance of us, coupled with his unabashed delight in us. Grace brings us adoption into God's family, a new identity, a new life, new power, new capacity, and God's full protection—with absolutely no strings attached! | But grace is much more than a theological position. Equally and simultaneously, grace is an actual environment, a realm, a present-tense reality that weaves around and through every moment of even our worst day. God's gift of grace continuously and always surrounds us. When we "approach the throne of grace," we are not coming to a throne made out of grace. The triune God lives in the realm of grace. Jesus, who lived on this earth, *came* full of grace and truth. Like any atmosphere, an environment of grace contains intangible, yet detectable, qualities. In this book we are explaining the particles that make up this atmosphere. You may not be able to see them—but you sure can feel them, just as you can detect whether you are breathing the air of a pine-filled forest or a smog-filled city. What a difference grace makes! |

*Trusting God means trusting that such a realm exists.*

You may have experienced grace as an environment in a counseling room. Many individuals who cannot detect a grace environment in their churches or organizations are referred to counselors. These counselors often provide safety, acceptance, and hope that we may not have sensed in our everyday environment. If this has been your experience, then you understand how grace works in an environment, in a relationship. And, you probably experienced a life-changing season, because grace environments help us mature.

(*TrueFaced*, pages 69-70)

From the preceding quotes, as well as your own experience, write down ways you can tell when you are in an environment or a relationship of grace.

What is it that gives us the confidence to approach a holy God in our unholy state? (See Hebrews 4:16.)

What is it that gives us the confidence to remove our masks before him? (See 2 Corinthians 3:18.)

**9.** When we live in The Room of Grace, we begin to relate to others differently. We begin to experience true intimacy. Do you know why? For the same reason we no longer have distance between God and us. Grace wonderfully reorients all our relationships. (*TrueFaced*, page 71)

Recall two different environments you have experienced, one that you remember as being guarded and hidden, the other characterized by grace and authenticity. Then check anything below that you experienced in each of those environments.

| In my room of authenticity, I . . . | In my room of hidden-ness, I . . . |
|---|---|
| ☐ showed my true face to others | ☐ saw others through a grid of shame, blame, and anger |
| ☐ felt safe and protected | ☐ competed with others |
| ☐ saw others as saints who sin | ☐ felt condemned and unaccepted |
| ☐ felt honored when others let me in on their struggles and pain | ☐ hid my real face from others |
| ☐ wanted to protect and help others | ☐ felt guardedness and deceit |
| ☐ felt God right there, maturing us | ☐ saw others as sinners trying to be saintly |
| ☐ felt relief prompted by the words, "What if they knew?" | ☐ felt embarrassed or helpless when others shared their struggles and pain with me |
| ☐ Other? | ☐ wanted others to fix their flaws themselves, or else get professional help |
| | ☐ felt we were performing our way to God |
| | ☐ felt fear prompted by the words, "What if they knew?" |
| | ☐ Other? |

How has the impact of those rooms affected your identity?

Describe a time when you found grace in a person or in a group that allowed you to shed your mask and be authentic about who and what you really were.

**10.** God's final objective for us is not resolving sin or "getting well." God's ultimate goal is maturing us into who he says we are, and then releasing us into the dreams he designed for us before the world began. . . . God carefully designed his "influence system" so that we would have to influence far more out of who we are than what we do. Therefore, God's "influence system" requires personal maturity. Do you see why God so deeply wants us to mature into the "likeness of his Son"? There is no profound influence without it. . . . The ultimate goal of grace is not resolving our sin, because maturing and destiny are the endgame. God's dreams for us are the ultimate goal. (*TrueFaced*, pages 74-75)

Why do you think maturity is critically important for having influence in God's kingdom? Why is immaturity critically dangerous?

Consider those who have influenced your life because:

. . . they were mature — What was the effect of their influence?

. . . they were immature — What was the effect of their influence?

# Experiencing TrueFaced Together

## Before you begin:

**1.** Get together with your group. If you are a part of a large group (such as a church school class), your teacher or leader will facilitate the experience. If you're doing this in a small-group setting, anyone can lead the group by following the directions in this section.

**2.** Consider the following guidelines for making the most of your group experience:

- When you are directed to form a small group for an activity, select people you know at least a little. If you are placed in a pair or trio with people you don't know, take a couple minutes to introduce yourselves. This will give you a good starting place for today's experiential activity.
- Follow the directions carefully, particularly as they relate to discussion in your small group. These directions have been designed to provide safe boundaries so you can share appropriately with others.
- The skills, techniques, and truths you discover during this experience are applicable in many other areas of life. Practice what you learn outside of small-group time.
- Above all, don't be anxious about the experiential activities in this guide. They aren't scary, "stand up in front of the group and share your life" experiences. Each Experiencing TrueFaced Together activity has been field-tested and is designed to ease you into participation. That's not to say what you learn will be fluffy, surface-level stuff. The experiences can be life-changing. We'll lead you into the deeper stuff. But come prepared to invest yourself in the experience. It will be worth it.

## For the Group Leader

If you are the designated leader for this TrueFaced Experience, please follow these guidelines to ensure a positive experience for all participants.

**1.** Make sure everyone has the necessary materials before the session. Each person should have a copy of *TrueFaced* and a copy of the *TrueFaced Experience Guide*. You'll also need a copy of the *TrueFaced Experience DVD* set for your group. This session uses DVD #2.

**2.** Review the DVD contents for each session and know right where to go to play them. Test your DVD player setup to avoid technical glitches.

**3.** You are a facilitator for this, not a teacher. Follow the instructions closely and fight any temptation to expand on the material provided. This is a place for experiential learning, *not* lecture.

**4.** Don't worry if some questions are left unanswered. Unanswered questions are part of the discovery process.

**5.** Close the session with prayer, and then remind participants of their homework assignments for the coming session.

## Safety

### Welcome

Take a moment to greet one another. If you traditionally enjoy snacks with your group, have at 'em. Use the opening moments as people congregate for a brief time of fellowship.

### Video Introduction

Gather in front of the TV/monitor and watch the video introduction to this session. It's called "Week 4: Safety/Acceptance" in your DVD menu

### Introducing the Experience

Today we're going to apply TrueFaced principles in an activity we call "Accepting Others." This process helps us experience acceptance in The Room of Grace. Acceptance is a principle of grace, which promotes truth-telling. As we share our individual journeys of moving into The Room of Grace, this experience helps us both offer and receive safety. This experience can transform your relationships.

### For an Enjoyable Experience

In order to make this experience excellent and beneficial to all, consider the following guidelines for your small- and large-group time:

- Allow the sharing members of the group to *discover*. Do not make them defend their statements as a final declaration of fact. This is part of experiencing safety.
- Allow the sharing members of the group to be *accepted*, not critiqued, counseled, or judged. This is part of experiencing truth-telling.

## About the DVD

To experience a life free of mask wearing, I must see grace as more than a polite, ethereal, religious concept. For many, grace is not much more than a nice reminder that God did some things we don't deserve. But grace is larger, more breathtaking than any of our wildest conceptions. Grace is a realm, a way of relating to each other, a way of seeing our relationship with God, a condition where I am finally comfortable and at rest, in my own skin. Embracing grace with both hands changes everything.

Among 27 trillion other benefits, grace changes our life focus, it allows God to truly solve our sin, it melts the very fabric of our masks and it changes how we treat each other when we sin. It also allows us to experience a truly wonderful state: *safety*.

Those who've been shaped by grace best shape the world. Any substitute robs, tires, weakens, and darkens, making me afraid and searching for a better fitting mask. This session may challenge our previous understandings about grace and leave us willing to let go of any lesser dream we've been clinging to in order to drink from her well. Get this one right, understand this one, make this your life's pursuit in Jesus and you'll be playing a ten-penny-tin-whistle in your heart, for the rest of your life.

*[John introduces Sue.]*

Jesus and I came together when I was 28. Into our relationship, I brought with me many years of highly skilled self-protection. Sarcasm was the tool I used most often. One day, a woman sat me down and said to me, "Sue, I see a lot of fear in your life. If you ever decide you want to take a look at it, I will help you." What was she talking about? I got on the phone to one of my closer friends. "What does she mean?" I asked. Then I heard these words. "Sue, she is talking about control." I think I was almost glad to be found out.

With the help of these friends I felt safe enough to begin to ask: Why was I this way? I began remembering things I had not remembered for many, many years. I remembered a time when I was sexually molested. This began a season when shame began to define me. I sought relationships that would prove I was worthy. I tried traveling. I pursued ambition and wealth.

Ultimately, God answered my questions through dear friends who were able to synergistically, with Him, estimate me with divine worth. I was listened to so well—gosh, they were patient— my friends began to know why I acted the way I did, they knew when I would be frightened and act out, and they responded to my heart with gentleness. I was accepted here. I was wanted. I was loved.

## The "Accepting Others" Experience

**1.** Begin by forming a small group with one or two partners. Groups of three work best. This experience should take approximately 30 minutes.

**2.** On your own, think about and write answers to the "Accepting Others Questions" in the next section.

**3.** After everyone's finished writing, take turns sharing your answers with your small group. Allow no more than five minutes per group member for this sharing time.

**4.** When everyone has shared, pray for each another. During the next several weeks process what you've discovered with trusted friends.

## Accepting Others Questions

**1.** What is your greatest concern in accepting people in The Room of Grace who you know still sin? (You will think of specific people but please don't mention names.)

**2.** What do you think you need to do differently in these relationships? How can you change your actions to imitate God's actions in your relationships with Christians who sin? (Remember, motives lead to values, and values lead to actions.)

**3.** What might it cost you if you did what you think you need to do?

**4.** You can invite others in your group to suggest a new question for you to answer. This can be risky, but very rewarding. You choose whether to answer it or one of the questions provided.

Notes:

## Processing the "Accepting Others" Experience

Form one large group and discuss the following question for no more than three minutes: *What did you just experience?* Allow time for everyone who so desires to respond. Stay focused on the processing question and use the guidelines outlined previously to facilitate a healthy discussion.

## Closing Video and Prayer

After exploring the processing question together, play the video segment called "Week 4: Safety/Acceptance Recap" on your DVD menu. Following this, close in prayer and review the homework for next week's session.

---

### About the DVD

We highly recommend you use the DVD for your TrueFaced Experience as it adds a significant dimension to the study. However, if you don't have access to this DVD, you can alternately have someone read aloud the summary that follows.

**John Lynch:** This experience was about giving safety. It was about applying these truths in an imperfect environment, where people fail and things get messy. It is absolutely fine to discover yourself not being so gracious in The Room of Grace— The Room of Grace makes allowances for our failing to accept those who fail.

We are painting a watercolor that is not just about solving this or that issue, painting this tree or that bush. This is about a way of seeing that evolves through applying washes of grace, truth, and love onto a variety of life interactions, until the painting is rich and warm and complete.

Have a great week, friends.

## Before the Next Session

Read chapter 4, "The Supreme Gift of Grace: Love," in your *TrueFaced* book. Then complete the "Experiencing TrueFaced on Your Own" section for Week Five in this Experience Guide (go to page 79). Pray throughout the week that your discoveries will positively impact all aspects of your everyday life.

# Introducing the Tool

If you want to go deeper with your TrueFaced experience, take time in the coming week to complete the "Accepting Others Tool" on your own. This tool gives you an opportunity to actually *act* on the truths in *TrueFaced*. Character is formed as we *act on truth* that touches our hearts. Acting is how we know we are *trusting* the truth. After you have completed your part of the exercise, share it with one or two trusted friends. (It's important that your friends read the corresponding chapter in *TrueFaced* so they can fully understand the process you are experiencing. Share your copy of *TrueFaced* or encourage them to buy a copy for themselves.)

## Accepting Others Tool

**1.** How do your actions in The Room of Grace encourage your friends to become truth-tellers about their unresolved sin?

**2.** What (if any) of your actions might cause them to want to leave The Room of Grace for The Room of Good Intentions? What could you change that might woo them back?

**3.** What actions might you take to reach one or more of your friends in The Room of Good Intentions and to invite them into The Room of Grace?

**4.** Now act on these answers to the three questions above. Share your action intentions with your trusted friends to help you follow through.

# Week Five: Love

# Experiencing TrueFaced on Your Own

## Before you begin:

**1.** Read chapter 4, "The Supreme Gift of Grace: Love" in your *TrueFaced* book. Take time to soak up all the stories and thoughts. This will be the basis for answering the following questions. You may want to review the "Did You Discover?" questions at the end of the chapter as well. To dig even further into the background for this chapter, look up the related Scripture passages referenced in the back of the *TrueFaced* book in the "Notes" section.

**2.** Get out a pen or pencil and respond to the questions that follow. Keep in mind this is your personal workbook for examining the truths in *TrueFaced*. It's okay to spill the truth onto these pages: they are "for your eyes only." Let this become a journal of your exploration of what it means to be TrueFaced.

## Love

**1.** Grace is the face that love wears, when it meets imperfection. . . . When you enter The Room of Grace, Jesus has some gifts for you. Gifts for every occasion and every need. They are given for the asking, to meet your specific needs. For every issue, every unresolved sin, every wound, God has created a gift specifically to meet that need, resolve that sin, and heal that wound. . . . Love, the first gift of grace, acts as a solvent to lift our masks. It acts as a balm that can begin to heal our unresolved sin so that we never want to put on a mask again. Those who receive this gift live in profound and sacred health . . . without fail . . . always. (*TrueFaced*, pages 83-84)

Let's unwrap the first grace gift — Love — by reading 1 John 4:16-19.

> God is love. When we take up permanent residence in a life
> of love, we live in God and God lives in us. This way, love has
> the run of the house, becomes at home and mature in us. . . .
> There is no room in love for fear. Well-formed love banishes
> fear. Since fear is crippling, a fearful life — fear of death,
> fear of judgment — is one not yet fully formed in love. We,
> though, are going to love — love and be loved. First we were
> loved, now we love. He loved us first. (MSG)

What are your early memories of receiving human love? Of receiving God's love?

Even the best of human love isn't perfect. Don's version of love (*TrueFaced*, page 84), for instance, felt to his family like "arrogance packaged as teaching;

control disguised as protection; manipulation wrapped as concern; exploitation marketed as opportunities." Until Don learned to *be* loved, his "loving" just spewed all of his unresolved junk and debris onto others. Are your memories of receiving love from others (either early in life or more recently) more like Don's version? Explain.

**2.** You may not have thought much about the art of receiving love, especially if you have been the recipient of degenerated love like Don's. But many of us actually find that hard to do. This chapter explores the process of receiving love, which we have broken down into seven steps. These steps are not some magic formula to be followed, but rather a description of what is going on in our hearts as we mature in the critical area of allowing ourselves to be loved. As you go through these steps, imagine how each one leads naturally to the next. Also pay attention to how your heart responds to each step.

Here's the first step: **Understand that I have needs.**

Many of us are all over the map when it comes to understanding what we *really* need. We are sure we need a new flat-screen monitor and a DSL line, but are equally convinced that we don't really need affirmation from our peers or advice on a difficult decision. Take this little "Needs Awareness" survey by placing these twelve items on the scale to reflect what you feel you need.

| I Don't Need This at All | Nice, but Not Necessary | I Want This | I Need This | This Is an Important Need | This Is a Critically Important Need |
|---|---|---|---|---|---|
| | | | | | |

a. A vacation

b. Increased income

c. Less stress

d. Better physical fitness

e. To be accepted

f. Affirmation by peers

g. Someone's advice on a decision

h. Someone's counsel on a personal struggle

i. Attention/listening from spouse or close friend

j. Time alone with God

k. Deeper connecting/communication at home

l. Help overcoming an unhealthy addiction

Look at the needs you identified as Important or Critically Important. Which ones are not being addressed in your priorities? Explain. Now identify someone you could ask to assist you in addressing those important needs.

**3.** Here is step two: **Having my needs met is experiencing love.**

Why did God create us with needs? Most of us have never thought about this before: Without needs we cannot experience love—we cannot know when we are being loved. . . . Needs give us the capacity to feel loved. We know or experience love when our needs are met. This is why we say that love is the process of meeting needs. (*TrueFaced*, pages 86-87)

Have you ever tried to offer someone help, only to be told (whether in words or actions), "I don't need help!" If so, how did you feel? What happened to the concern, compassion, and love that motivated you to offer your help in the first place? What does this tell you about the purpose of having needs?

Think of a time when you were experiencing a critical need—perhaps for comfort, or protection, or support, or whatever. Did someone step forward to help meet that need? Describe how that felt. How did you respond?

**4.** And now the third step: **I freely admit that I long to be loved.**

Remember Rick, the graduate student who insisted that he had no needs so he wouldn't have to risk being loved—and perhaps being hurt—again (*TrueFaced*, page 87)?

Has there been a time when you walked a path similar to Rick's? What strategies did you adopt to protect yourself?

Rick's pain occurred when he was divorced. Do you have a divorced or a widowed friend who has needs for acceptance, security, affirmation, child-care, practical assistance—or maybe just a hug—that *you* could meet, at least for an hour or two? Consider making yourself available to meet a need in this person's life this week.

Perhaps your whole small group could adopt a divorced or widowed acquaintance and corporately address a significant need in this person's life.

**5.** On to step four: **I *let* you love me.**

The degree to which I let you love me is the degree to which you can love me, no matter how much love you have for me. . . . We cannot let another person love us unless we trust the person. People who are unable to trust will never experience love. Ever. . . . Many people who deeply want to be loved are not loved, because they won't turn that doorknob of Humility— "trusting God and others with me." They stand out in the cold, outside The Room of Grace, in pain (and blame) because people don't love them. . . . The people God wants to use to love you deeply and to meet your needs stand right on the other side of that door. Turn the knob. (*TrueFaced*, pages 90-91)

According to this quote, and from your own experience:

> a. Why do you think it is so difficult for some of us to let others love us?

> b. In order to receive your love, I must trust you. Agree or disagree? Explain.

> c. In order to receive your love, I must be humble. Agree or disagree? Explain.

> d. Who is receiving your love?

> e. Whose love are you receiving?

**6.** Step five states: **I let you love me on your terms—not mine.**

Do you have a friend who struggles with a weakness that is one of your strengths? For example:

- an introverted friend who needs you to initiate social contacts
- a reluctant friend who needs you to open a door to release his or her leadership skills
- a procrastinating friend who needs you to jump-start a needed process or help bring closure to a decision
- a stressed-out friend who needs you to suggest creative rest or other boundaries
- a task-oriented friend who needs you to shed light on people issues or feelings
- Other?

What initiative do you sense God nudging you to take to love this friend by meeting his or her need?

Now think about someone close to you—someone you love.

- What are one or two of this person's current needs or weaknesses?
- What are one or two practical ways you might meet those needs or come alongside to strengthen those weaknesses?
- How will you handle potential reluctance to your offer of love?

**7.** On to step six: **I am fulfilled when I experience love.**

Try to identify one current pain or longing that you are dealing with. Don't fret over its "size." No pain is too big or too small. Just summarize it here.

You may be feeling discouraged at this point, wondering where these ideal friends of yours are. Maybe nobody's lining up even to think about your needs, much less rushing to meet them. Perhaps the last couple of times you dared mention a need, you were disappointed. Read these verses and summarize the encouragement they give you to rely on God's love for your fulfillment:

- Deuteronomy 7:7-9
- Deuteronomy 33:12
- 2 Timothy 2:13
- 1 John 4:18

**8.** And finally, we reach step seven: **I am now able to love others out of my own fulfillment.**

Having our needs met by receiving the love of God and others is not just about "feeling better"; it's about fulfillment. To *fulfill* means "to meet the requirements of, to satisfy." When the requirements of our soul—our needs—are met, it satisfies us. This fulfillment produces inward peace, contentment, and healing for our wounds. As our wounds heal, we can turn away from them with a fresh passion, confidence, and love for others. (*TrueFaced*, page 95)

What are the "requirements" of our soul? What do you think it might look like for you to receive the love of God and find those requirements satisfied?

**9.** Millions of people have yet to meet the King of Love. When they see us living in blame, shame, fear, denial, and anger, with no real answers, it confuses them. When they see us attempting to mask those dysfunctions, it tells them not to trust us—or the God we follow. When they see us focused on wounds that never heal, they conclude we cannot deal with theirs. That's a major reason why life in The Room of Good Intentions is such a waste. It never produces an environment conducive to people courageously attempting their first footsteps of trusting the grace and love of Jesus Christ. (*TrueFaced*, pages 95-96)

Narrow your focus from the millions down to the handful of people in your sphere of influence who have yet to meet the King of Love. How does your life right now move or cause them to experience love? Explain.

# Experiencing TrueFaced Together

## Before you begin:

**1.** Get together with your group. If you are a part of a large group (such as a church school class), your teacher or leader will facilitate the experience. If you're doing this in a small-group setting, anyone can lead the group by following the directions in this section.

**2.** Consider the following guidelines for making the most of your group experience:

- When you are directed to form a small group for an activity, select people you know at least a little. If you are placed in a pair or trio with people you don't know, take a couple minutes to introduce yourselves. This will give you a good starting place for today's experiential activity.
- Follow the directions carefully, particularly as they relate to discussion in your small group. These directions have been designed to provide safe boundaries so you can share appropriately with others.
- The skills, techniques, and truths you discover during this experience are applicable in many other areas of life. Practice what you learn outside of small-group time.
- Above all, don't be anxious about the experiential activities in this guide. They aren't scary, "stand up in front of the group and share your life" experiences. Each Experiencing TrueFaced Together activity has been field-tested and is designed to ease you into participation. That's not to say what you learn will be fluffy, surface-level stuff. The experiences can be life-changing. We'll lead you into the deeper stuff. But come prepared to invest yourself in the experience. It will be worth it.

## For the Group Leader

If you are the designated leader for this TrueFaced Experience, please follow these guidelines to ensure a positive experience for all participants.

**1.** Make sure everyone has the necessary materials before the session. Each person should have a copy of *TrueFaced* and a copy of the *TrueFaced Experience Guide*. You'll also need a copy of the *TrueFaced Experience DVD* set for your group. This session uses DVD #2.

**2.** Review the DVD contents for each session and know right where to go to play them. Test your DVD player setup to avoid technical glitches.

**3.** You are a facilitator for this, not a teacher. Follow the instructions closely and fight any temptation to expand on the material provided. This is a place for experiential learning, *not* lecture.

**4.** Don't worry if some questions are left unanswered. Unanswered questions are part of the discovery process.

**5.** Close the session with prayer, and then remind participants of their homework assignments for the coming session.

# Love

## Welcome

Take a moment to greet one another. If you traditionally enjoy snacks with your group, have at 'em. Use the opening moments as people congregate for a brief time of fellowship.

## Video Introduction

Gather in front of the TV/monitor and watch the video introduction to this session. It's called "Week 5: Love/Permission" in your DVD menu. Then move to the "Introducing the Experience" section.

## Introducing the Experience

Today we're going to apply TrueFaced principles in an activity we call "Granting Permission." Love is a process of choosing to let others meet your needs—on their terms, not yours. One of the most profound steps in learning to receive love in The Room of Grace is *granting permission to others to meet my needs*.

## For an Enjoyable Experience

In order to make this experience excellent and beneficial to all, consider the following guidelines for your small- and large-group time:

- Allow the sharing group members to *discover*. Do not make them defend their statements as a final declaration of fact. This is part of experiencing safety.
- Allow the sharing group members to be *accepted*, not critiqued, counseled, or judged. This is part of experiencing truth-telling.

## About the DVD

We highly recommend you use the DVD for your TrueFaced Experience as it adds a significant dimension to the study. John Lynch is your DVD host and offers lots of good thoughts and compelling real-life stories that can help you in your journey. However, if you don't have access to the DVD, you can alternately have someone read aloud John's abbreviated introduction that follows.

**John Lynch:** Many of us have never experienced love because we have been terrified to give another person permission to love us. We allow them to be loved by us, but somewhere along the line we equated permission with giving someone control over us. Few of us know how to allow ourselves to be loved. This experience into permission may feel at first like being pushed into a vat of ice water! But in truth, some of us have been so cold, hiding from love, that we reckon it couldn't be much colder. So we are ready to take the risk. Permission is one of the great love words. It opens the door to so much we long for.

*[John introduces Wendy, who is the person referred to as Andrea in* TrueFaced.*]*

**Wendy's Story:** I grew up with the world's two greatest parents and the ultimate rarity—a truly functional family. But my perfect world was shattered when my mother died suddenly. My mom was in no way responsible for her untimely death, but I realized I needed to protect myself so I would never, ever be that hurt again. I become totally self-sufficient.

One day I stumbled into a new church where the preacher dressed in tennis shoes. When he started his stand-up comedy routine, I embarrassed myself by laughing out loud, but later had tears pouring down my face. God was obviously speaking to me directly through the person of John Lynch.

In our subsequent conversations, John made it so clear that my personal understanding was important to him that I was willing to expose my spiritual ignorance. I granted John permission to teach me spiritual truth, and as I learned to trust him, he was able to influence my life.

God didn't create us to live in isolation. You may or may not have a John Lynch in your life. But you need to find one or two. At times they may say or do dim-witted things, but if you give them permission in your life, God can use them powerfully in your journey.

## The "Granting Permission" Experience

**1.** Begin by forming a small group with one or two partners. Groups of three work best. This experience should take approximately 30 minutes.

**2.** On your own, think about and write answers to the "Granting Permission Questions" in the next section.

**3.** After everyone's finished writing, take the next twenty minutes or so to talk together in your small group about your answers.

**4.** After your discussion time, pray together.

## Granting Permission Questions

**1.** What, relationally speaking, must be in place before you grant someone permission to speak to or protect you in a specific life area?

**2.** Granting permission in friendships, marriages, families, workplaces, schools, and churches is not very common. Why do you think that is?

**3.** What are some of the benefits for individuals, families, and teams if people actively practiced granting permission to each other?

**4.** Identify one person that you might grant permission to in a specific area of your life. What must happen for you to do this?

**5.** You can invite others in your group to suggest a new question for you to answer. This can be risky, but very rewarding. You choose whether to answer it or one of the questions provided.

### More Love

Granting permission is the most *profound* way to receive love and protection for our limitations, weaknesses, and unresolved sin issues. But this process may be difficult for you. An easier way to receive love is through affirmation. If you want to learn how to experience affirmation, check out Leadership Catalyst's widely used Affirmation Tools for individuals, marriages, and families on our website (www.leadershipcatalyst.org).

### Notes:

## Processing the "Granting Permission" Experience

Form one large group and discuss the following question for no more than three minutes: *What did you just experience?* Allow time for everyone who so desires to respond. Stay focused on the processing question and use the guidelines outlined previously to facilitate a healthy discussion.

## Closing Video and Prayer

After exploring the processing question together, play the video segment called "Week 5: Love/Permission Recap" on your DVD menu. Following this, close in prayer and review the homework for next week's session.

## Before the Next Session

Read chapter 5, "The Sweetest Gift of Grace: Repentance," in your *TrueFaced* book. Then complete the "Experiencing TrueFaced on Your Own" section for Week Six in this Experience Guide (go to page 97). Pray throughout the week that your discoveries will positively impact all aspects of your everyday life.

---

## About the DVD

We highly recommend you use the DVD for your TrueFaced Experience as it adds a significant dimension to the study. However, if you don't have access to this DVD, you can alternately have someone read aloud the summary that follows.

**John Lynch:** Welcome back. So, how did it go? We hope you actually did "identify one person that you might grant permission to in a specific area of your life." That choice alone begins an incredible new experience. What you will discover, once you give this permission, is love pouring over you for the purpose of meeting deep and longing needs.

When you tell that "one person" that you would like to grant them permission into a specific area of your life, they will smile and think to themselves, "Oh yes! Finally, I get to love this one I've longed to love for so long. Thank you, God." And they will want to treat your permission with honor and sacred care, treasuring your trust.

---

# Introducing the Tool

If you want to go deeper with your TrueFaced experience, take time in the coming week to complete the "Granting Permission Tool" on your own. This tool gives you an opportunity to actually *act* on the truths in *TrueFaced*. Character is formed as we *act on truth* that touches our hearts. Acting is how we know we are *trusting* the truth. After you have completed your part of the exercise, share it with one or two trusted friends. (It's important that your friends read the corresponding chapter in *TrueFaced* so they can fully understand the process you are experiencing. Share your copy of *TrueFaced* or encourage them to buy a copy for themselves.)

## Granting Permission Tool

Receiving love by granting permission to someone else requires an act of trust. That trust triggers the biblical concept of submission.

**1.** Identify one to three people to whom you will consider granting permission for the purpose of guarding specific limitations and weaknesses. Note the specific limitation or weakness you will entrust with each person. (Choose people who are strong in the areas where you are weak.)

- _____
- _____
- _____

Example: One of the *TrueFaced* coauthors grants his twenty-something daughter permission to protect him in his impatience, grants his teenage son permission to guard his tendency toward lack of compassion, and grants his administrative assistant permission to guard against overload.

**2.** Set the date by which time you will grant the appropriate permission to at least two of these people on your list. Share the date with your friends.

**3.** Now, do it! This could be a wonderful milestone day in your life.

The practice of granting someone else permission to protect your limitations is a powerful way to build trust, maturity, character, team effectiveness, and leadership qualities.

# Week Six: Freedom

# Experiencing TrueFaced on Your Own

## Before you begin:

**1.** Read chapter 5, "The Sweetest Gift of Grace: Repentance" in your *TrueFaced* book. Take time to soak up all the stories and thoughts. This will be the basis for answering the following questions. You may want to review the "Did You Discover?" questions at the end of the chapter as well. To dig even further into the background for this chapter, look up the related Scripture passages referenced in the back of the *TrueFaced* book in the "Notes" section.

**2.** Get out a pen or pencil and respond to the questions that follow. Keep in mind this is your personal workbook for examining the truths in *TrueFaced*. It's okay to spill the truth onto these pages: they are "for your eyes only." Let this become a journal of your exploration of what it means to be TrueFaced.

# Freedom

**1.** When grace brings truth to light, it sometimes does so through love (as we learned in the last chapter), sometimes through forgiveness (as we'll learn in the next chapter), and sometimes through repentance. The principles of God's grace play off of each other. Grace begets repentance, and repentance nurtures forgiveness. Trust attracts grace, and grace helps saints to trust. Even goofed-up, compromised, failed, and confused saints. *Especially* them. When repentance becomes a constant, recognizable part in an environment, the people in that culture experience freedom they never knew. They have amazing stories to tell. The truth always sets us free. Free to love God and others, free to trust even more truth, free to heal and reconcile, free to bring reconciliation to those who still don't know the Reconciler, free to follow our callings and dreams. (*TrueFaced*, page 111)

But when we walk around with unresolved sin, it's as if we're wearing a heavily insulated parka on the hottest day of the summer . . . in the Sahara! We're suffocating and can't figure out why. Repentance is the zipper out of that parka. (*TrueFaced*, page 99)

What a great image for what repentance feels like! Try your hand at defining repentance with a similar word picture:
If we're . . .


. . . then repentance is . . .

**2.** When we don't know how to deal with our sin, we will try to hide it. That's why The Room of Good Intentions turns into such a masquerade ball. It's dress-up time! We know what we've done . . . we know what we *do*. And no amount of sadness, striving, or penance has done anything but compound our sadness. What we really need is a way home. We've been told to confess our sin, but we don't like that answer. We want to do something! Besides, we've confessed our sin a thousand times before, and what good did it do? (*TrueFaced*, page 99)

For several chapters, we've looked at alternative ways to deal with our sin, all ultimately ineffective. From those chapters and from the quote above, what are some of those ways?

Here are three more ways to deal with sin:

- Remorse—Bitter regret or moral anguish arising from repentance for past misdeeds.
- Mortification—A feeling of shame, humiliation, or wounded pride.
- Penance—A voluntary act of humiliating yourself in order to express sorrow for sin.

Why are all of these ways ultimately ineffective?

**3.** Confess . . . do better for a while, then sin again. Embarrassment, confess again, ask God to take away the desire, then sin again, confess again, sin again, confess again, shock, more determination to stop sinning, think about it a lot, examine it. Make promises, create some boundaries, and sin again, now even worse than before. Despair, anger, shame, distance from God, guilt. Self-condemnation, self-loathing . . . sin again. Disillusionment, doubt, self-pity, resentment at God: *Why doesn't he hear my prayers? Why doesn't he do something?* More anger. Then fear that we allow ourselves to get angry with God. Then real confession, a heartfelt one, and a sense of cleansing. Ah, a new start. Things seem better. *Yeah, I've finally got this sin under control.* Oops, sin again. Desperate efforts, bargains struck. Once-and-for-all healing. Really mean it this time. Sin again. Lose hope, give up, rationalize, minimize, blame, pull away, hide, judge others, put on a mask, go past the sin again, and so on. (*TrueFaced*, pages 101-102)

Does this approach to sin management sound familiar to you? Has there been a time when you tried—really tried—to end a bad habit or stop committing a reoccurring sin, but you failed? Is so, describe it. Has *TrueFaced* given you new hope? Why?

**4.** Yet many of us act as if repentance is a matter of the will. It's not. We cannot make a decision to stop sinning. We can't "will" ourselves into change. We can't "will" ourselves into feeling contrition or remorse. Repentance isn't doing something about our sin; rather, it means admitting that we *can't* do anything about our sin. We cannot woo ourselves into anything but the most external form of repentance. . . . Understand this: The *intention* not to sin is not the same as the *power* not to sin. God did not design us to conquer sin on our own. To think we can is an incalculable *under*valuing of sin's power combined with a huge overvaluing of our own willpower! Unfortunately, some of us fool ourselves into believing we can manage our sin, because we can stop from doing some things. Sometimes we learn to pick up our clothes after multiple reprimands . . . or we stop drinking diet soda after friends and relatives keep warning us of the ingredients . . . or we start driving the speed limit after our fifth speeding ticket. We think that because our will was sufficient enough to change some habits, we can tackle the big dog of sin. *Sin cannot be managed.* If we make this our goal in repentance, we are doomed to fail. (*TrueFaced*, pages 100-101)

Why do you think attempts at sin management ultimately fail? How are you left feeling when sin management fails . . . again?

**5.** Our goal isn't to solve all our sin issues. Our motive is to trust God so we can live out of who God says we are . . . so that *together* we can work on our sin issues. . . . Some may question, "How can repentance be a gift if I am the one who's doing the repenting?" It is a gift of God's grace because your repentance literally doesn't have a chance without grace. Grace alone resolves sin. Grace alone heals, and grace alone gives power over sin. Only the power of the Cross can break a pattern of sinful behavior. That's what makes repentance a gift that only Jesus can give. No one else died to bring us such power. (*TrueFaced*, pages 100-101)

We believe that the only effective way to deal with sin is repentance. What makes repentance a gift of God's grace instead of an act of my own willpower? Why is it effective when other strategies are not? Explain.

Study the passages below to discover the Bible's view of "sin management" and human willpower versus the powerful gift of grace in repentance. Note what you think is important from each passage:

- Isaiah 64:6

- Luke 18:14

- 1 John 1:7–2:2

**6.** When grace introduces us to repentance, the two of us become best friends. When anything else introduces us to repentance, it feels like the warden has come to lock us up. (*TrueFaced*, page 103)

But when grace gets involved [in the introductions], the truths of repentance reveal a fabulous world of life-freeing beauty. What, then, are the truths of repentance that grace produces? (*TrueFaced*, page 103)

To repent means to admit to myself, to God, and to selected others what is true about me—the whole truth. You can be shamed into repentance or dragged into a sort of repentance at the end of a guilt trip or an act of self-humiliation. But those are never the tactics of grace. Grace invites you to *receive repentance as a gift*. In the process, grace-empowered repentance actually resolves your sin, and thus sets you on the road to maturity. Here are five things that are true when grace produces repentance. These are five beautiful truths!

Truth #1:    Repentance is about trusting—not willing.

Truth #2:    Trusting God attracts grace's power to transform us, as we repent.

Truth #3:    Trusting God with ourselves allows us to receive unconditional love and feel safe enough to remove our masks in repentance.

Truth #4:    The safety we feel inclines us to stop defending ourselves, and it opens our hearts to God instead.

Truth #5:    Every act of repentance depends upon an act of redemption.

Select one of these truths and explain why it is a revolutionary way for you to see repentance.

Select one of these truths and explain what makes it such a beautiful gift for you to receive.

**7.** Meditate on the apostle Paul's words to Titus, describing what happens when we walk off the well-worn path of Pleasing God and start walking down the road of Trusting God.

It wasn't so long ago that we ourselves were stupid and stub
born, dupes of sin, ordered every which way by our glands
going around with a chip on our shoulder, hated and hatin
back. But when God, our kind and loving Savior God, steppe
in, he saved us from all that. It was all his doing; we ha
nothing to do with it. He gave us a good bath, and we cam
out of it new people, washed inside and out by the Hol
Spirit. Our Savior Jesus poured out new life so generousl
God's gift has restored our relationship with him and give
us back our lives. And there's more life to come — an eternit
of life! You can count on this. (Titus 3:3-7, MSG

In this Scripture, underline everything God does to resolve our sin issues
for us, then circle everything we do to resolve our sin issues for ourselves.
Meditate on these truths for a moment before continuing.

**8.** By now you know that people in The Room of Good Intentions hold
radically different assumptions about how to handle sin than those in The
Room of Grace. The environment of the first room actually inhibits repentance, while the second one releases it. Notice three specific inhibitors of
repentance. (*TrueFaced*, page 106)

Consider the three factors that can interfere with your move to repentance:
isolation, pride, and wrong motive. According to the authors and your own
observation, explain:

Why *isolation* inhibits your repentance.

How *pride* inhibits your repentance.

How *wrong motives* inhibit your repentance.

Now list two things that can lead you to repentance. (See Romans 2:4 and 2 Corinthians 7:10-11.)

**9.** Resolute striving to *please* God begets a pride that keeps us focused on our own "power"—which is not a power to write home about. In contrast, repentance that comes from God is outfitted with otherworldly power—potency secured by Jesus' death and activated by his resurrection. Repentance is formidable against sin only because of actual power—the power of the Cross. Our words or religious techniques have nothing to do with it. The power in this gift reminds us of the power in the ark of the covenant, a power so mighty that the Hebrews dared not come in contact with it. The same power that resided in the ark is the power in this gift. But now, God invites us to come near his grace-wrapped power. (*TrueFaced*, page 107)

What is more likely to inhibit *you* from opening the gift of repentance: isolation, pride, or wrong motive? Explain. Being aware of this weakness is a valuable insight. Pause to pray about it, inviting Grace to focus her awesome power in disarming your isolation, pride, or motives. Pray Romans 2:4 and 2 Corinthians 7:10-11 into the voids of your heart. Anticipate tasting how sweet repentance really is!

**10.** One day this woman stands near the door, waiting for the next wounded soul to stumble in, so she can be one of the first to tell the new story of this gift . . . a gift "used quite routinely in the community." When failing strivers stumble into a community of grace, safety, and vulnerable repentance, it radically disrupts their game plan. Suddenly, they are face to face with a real, tangible option of sweet freedom. And the·ongoing environment of the community tells them that they have not dreamed up this way of life. As the community treats them as they have never been treated before, their confidence grows that grace can support the full weight of their sin. (*TrueFaced*, page 109)

From the paragraph above, how can living in a community of grace affect someone? Underline several effects.

If you really believed that "grace can support the full weight of [your] sin," what would you do about it?

# Experiencing TrueFaced Together

## Before you begin:

**1.** Get together with your group. If you are a part of a large group (such as a church school class), your teacher or leader will facilitate the experience. If you're doing this in a small-group setting, anyone can lead the group by following the directions in this section.

**2.** Consider the following guidelines for making the most of your group experience:

- When you are directed to form a small group for an activity, select people you know at least a little. If you are placed in a pair or trio with people you don't know, take a couple minutes to introduce yourselves. This will give you a good starting place for today's experiential activity.
- Follow the directions carefully, particularly as they relate to discussion in your small group. These directions have been designed to provide safe boundaries so you can share appropriately with others.
- The skills, techniques, and truths you discover during this experience are applicable in many other areas of life. Practice what you learn outside of small-group time.
- Above all, don't be anxious about the experiential activities in this guide. They aren't scary, "stand up in front of the group and share your life" experiences. Each Experiencing TrueFaced Together activity has been field-tested and is designed to ease you into participation. That's not to say what you learn will be fluffy, surface-level stuff. The experiences can be life-changing. We'll lead you into the deeper stuff. But come prepared to invest yourself in the experience. It will be worth it.

## For the Group Leader

If you are the designated leader for this TrueFaced Experience, please follow these guidelines to ensure a positive experience for all participants.

**1.** Make sure everyone has the necessary materials before the session. Each person should have a copy of *TrueFaced* and a copy of the *TrueFaced Experience Guide*. You'll also need a copy of the *TrueFaced Experience DVD* set for your group. This session uses DVD #2.

**2.** Review the DVD contents for each session and know right where to go to play them. Test your DVD player setup to avoid technical glitches.

**3.** You are a facilitator for this, not a teacher. Follow the instructions closely and fight any temptation to expand on the material provided. This is a place for experiential learning, *not* lecture.

**4.** Don't worry if some questions are left unanswered. Unanswered questions are part of the discovery process.

**5.** Close the session with prayer, and then remind participants of their homework assignments for the coming session.

# Freedom

## Welcome

Take a moment to greet one another. If you traditionally enjoy snacks with your group, have at 'em. Use the opening moments as people congregate for a brief time of fellowship.

## Video Introduction

Gather in front of the TV/monitor and watch the video introduction to this session. It's called "Week 6: Freedom/Repentance" in your DVD menu.

---

### About the DVD

We highly recommend you use the DVD for your TrueFaced Experience as it adds a significant dimension to the study. John Lynch is your DVD host and offers lots of good thoughts and compelling real-life stories that can help you in your journey. However, if you don't have access to the DVD, you can alternately have someone read aloud John's abbreviated introduction that follows.

**John Lynch:** I have a sixteen-year-old daughter. I did not know that you could have as good a relationship with a daughter as I am enjoying with Amy. I'm not sure I would have always said that. But something happened that seemed to shape her path with great beauty and grace.

At times Amy has been in love with the thought of being in love. After her emotions cool, she backs away to "just being friends." She did this with this particular young man, and it hurt him. One morning I took her out for breakfast and bumbled my way into sharing my concern about her relationships. She immediately got defensive.

I was so sad because my daughter was choosing to go it alone. Somewhere in the middle of mixing eggs with my hash browns, I started to cry. Amy asked me what was wrong and I told her how sad it must make Jesus to watch her bluff through life alone, reacting and repositioning.

*Something beautiful happened in that moment. Trust awakened.*

That morning my precious daughter broke the pattern of an "I'm sorry" that gets parents off her back to an "I'm sorry" that demonstrates repentance. *In that moment, my precious daughter learned not to go it alone.*

We are going to return now to a somewhat familiar exercise. But this time, in the setting of trusted relationships, we are hoping to validate the freedom available in repentance. We will rehearse with each other past experiences where something other than real repentance short-circuited our freedom. Listen to each other. Protect each other with the truths you have been reminded of in this session. Friends, this is sacred ministry.

## Introducing the Experience

Today we're going to apply TrueFaced principles in an activity we call "Repenting." This experience helps us live in the freedom of the sweetest gift Jesus offers us in The Room of Grace—the gift of repentance. This gift is commonplace—it is used all the time in The Room of Grace, but seldom if ever in The Room of Good Intentions. Freedom is usually bought with power: We experience freedom when we trust that the power of the Cross is greater than the power of any sin.

## For an Enjoyable Experience

In order to make this experience excellent and beneficial to all, consider the following guidelines for your small- and large-group time:

- Bring a mindset that says, "I am for the other person's best."
- Allow other group members to answer their questions. Do not interrupt.
- Allow other group members to "keep" their answers. Do not correct.
- Allow other group members to share their answers. Do not counsel. Listening to others talk about their experiences is a wonderful affirmation for them.
- Allow other group members to experience safety. Do not discuss their answers outside your group, unless they give you permission to do so.

## The "Repenting" Experience

**1.** Begin by forming a small group with one or two partners. Groups of three work best. This experience should take approximately 30 minutes.

**2.** In your small group, have each person choose one of the questions in the "Repentance Questions" box. Each small-group member may answer any question— you don't have to all answer the same question although it's certainly okay if you do.

**3.** Take turns in your group sharing your answer to the question you've chosen. As others in your small group are talking, listen intently. Ask yourself "What am I learning?" not "What can I teach the others?" Consider what clarifying questions you might ask once a group member is done talking. Clarifying questions include: "What did you mean by . . . ," "How did that affect you . . . ," or "Did you say . . . " questions but not "Why" questions. You might want to jot these down in the "Notes" space.

**4.** After answering your question, have the rest of the group members each ask one clarifying question.

**5.** Pray for each group member after all clarifying questions have been answered. Then if you still have time, have each group member choose another question to answer and follow the same instructions.

## Repentance Questions

**1.** Have you experienced a time when repentance failed in The Room of Good Intentions? Explain.

**2.** Have you experienced repentance working when it was about *trusting*, not willpower? Explain.

**3.** What does it look like when people try to manage their sin?

**4.** When did you experience "freedom" as a result of personal repentance?

**5.** You can invite others in your group to suggest a new question for you to answer. This can be risky, but very rewarding. You choose whether to answer it or one of the questions provided.

## Notes:

## Processing the "Repenting" Experience

Form one large group and discuss the following question for no more than three minutes: *What did you just experience?* Allow time for everyone who so desires to respond. Stay focused on the processing question and use the guidelines outlined previously to facilitate a healthy discussion.

## Closing Video and Prayer

After exploring the processing question together, play the video segment called "Week 6: Freedom/Repentance Recap" on your DVD menu. Following this, close in prayer and review the homework for next week's session.

## Before the Next Session

Read chapter 6, "The Most Mysterious Gift of Grace: Forgiveness," in your *TrueFaced* book. Then complete the "Experiencing TrueFaced on Your Own" section for Week Seven in this Experience Guide (go to page 119). Pray throughout the week that your discoveries will positively impact all aspects of your everyday life.

## About the DVD

We highly recommend you use the DVD for your TrueFaced Experience as it adds a significant dimension to the study. However, if you don't have access to this DVD, you can alternately have someone read aloud the summary that follows.

**John Lynch:** Some of you have been examining a faulty view of repentance. You've tried willpower repentance for most of your Christian experience and it's only made you weary and discouraged. And now here we are telling you about the miraculous power and release of a trust-centered repentance. This is an incredible gift. It will just take some time to unwrap it.

May we make a suggestion? Find someone you love and ask him or her to sit down and listen to you reiterate what you are learning. Put it in your own language. Wrestle with it like a dog with a bone.

Try this stuff on and walk through your daily life with it. Pass it on to your family, your friends. It will revolutionize the way you live out your faith, see life, and face failure.

Have a great week!

# Introducing the Tool

If you want to go deeper with your TrueFaced experience, take time in the coming week to complete the "Repenting Tool" on your own. This tool gives you an opportunity to actually *act* on the truths in *TrueFaced*. Character is formed as we *act on truth* that touches our hearts. Acting is how we know we are *trusting* the truth. After you have completed your part of the exercise, share it with one or two trusted friends. (It's important that your friends read the corresponding chapter in *TrueFaced* so they can fully understand the process you are experiencing. Share your copy of *TrueFaced* or encourage them to buy a copy for themselves.)

## Repenting Tool

**1.** Describe the price you pay (and may be paying today) for resisting the heart change God wants you to make. Explain this price in one or more of the following areas:

- Relational (loss of intimacy with God and others, loss of influence, loss of opportunities)

- Spiritual/Emotional (spiritual dryness, loss of focus, pain, lack of healing, loss of creativity, heaviness, sense of imprisonment)

- Physical (sleep loss, energy loss, illness)

- Circumstantial (financial, job or asset loss)

**2.** Describe the price you believe you would have to pay for receiving the grace of repentance. Explain this price in one or more of the following ways:

- Giving up control in a relationship
- Giving up your hurt
- Trusting God and others instead of yourself
- Acknowledging you were wrong

**3.** Which "prices" do you want to continue paying, those from question 1 or question 2? (If you choose question 2, don't attempt to "will yourself" into this experience. Repentance is a *gift*. *When* you trust the gift, you *receive* it. This one gift alone can change your life. So trust God's view of what you should do and enjoy the *rest* and the *freedom* that comes with this gift—the freedom to be in a position where your relationship with God and others can begin to be restored.)

**4.** As you receive this gift, *follow God into the action* for which you are trusting him. If you do not know for sure what he is asking, ask your trusted friends if they have thoughts or counsel for you.

# Week Seven: Healing

# Experiencing TrueFaced on Your Own

## Before you begin:

**1.** Read chapter 6, "The Most Mysterious Gift of Grace: Forgiveness" in your *TrueFaced* book. Take time to soak up all the stories and thoughts. This will be the basis for answering the following questions. You may want to review the "Did You Discover?" questions at the end of the chapter as well. To dig even further into the background for this chapter, look up the related Scripture passages referenced in the back of the *TrueFaced* book in the "Notes" section.

**2.** Get out a pen or pencil and respond to the questions that follow. Keep in mind this is your personal workbook for examining the truths in *TrueFaced*. It's okay to spill the truth onto these pages: they are "for your eyes only." Let this become a journal of your exploration of what it means to be TrueFaced.

# Healing

**1.** We need a way home. We've been told to get over the sin done to us, but we can't find our way out of the shadows. We can't seem to let go of our hurt. (*TrueFaced*, page 117)

This chapter leads us home again! As you begin unwrapping grace's most mysterious gift—forgiveness—it will help you to glance briefly back into the shadows. That's where you've stored the insidious harm and pain that came when sin was done against you. For a few moments, *remember*. List three sins, or offenses, committed against you, whether intentionally or inadvertently. If this is difficult for you, think of three times when you experienced hurt. Also put specific words to the pain you felt at the time, including painful consequences that followed later. An example is provided for you. (You will be referring to these three offenses throughout the chapter.)

## Example

**Offense:** I reported to my boss about the unethical business behavior of a coworker, and instead of the coworker being disciplined, I got fired.

Pain and Consequences:

- I felt *betrayed* by a boss I had trusted and liked
- *unjust* and *unfair* that the culprit got to keep her job
- *humiliation* and *embarrassment* of being fired
- *sorrow* over leaving good friends at that workplace
- *angry* and *worried* that this is a bad mark on my resume for future professional advancement
- *financial hardship* my family had to endure until I found another job
- made me *cynical* and *hardened* ("Just keep your mouth shut from now on.")
- I *have trouble trusting* authority figures
- makes me *want to turn a blind eye* to unethical practices—and that makes me feel *guilty*

| Sin or Offense Against You | Pain and Consequences |
|---|---|
| 1. | |
| 2. | |
| 3. | |

Don't continue until you have listed three offenses, especially any that still cause you pain to think about.

**2.** Forgiveness is a process with several steps. Jumping to the last steps without attending to the first steps will probably leave critical issues unresolved. Number these steps of forgiveness in the order you think will bring the healthiest long-term resolution.

___ Forgive the consequences of the act done against you.

___ Distinguish between forgiving and trusting your offender.

___ Tell God what happened to you.

_1_ Admit something happened.

___ Seek reconciliation, not just conflict resolution.

___ Forgive the offender (when he or she repents) for *their* sake.

___ Forgive the offender for *your* sake.

**3.** You read the story of Bill's high school "friends" stripping him naked in the stairwell as a practical joke (*TrueFaced*, page 118). Of course, this caused him incredible embarrassment, pain, and shame at the time. But the damage didn't stop there. Even after moving away, his trauma allowed those sins' inevitable effects to gang up on him.

Now he was angry, and his anger had an immensely profound effect. Bill began to blame that experience for why he didn't know how to get along with girls. He'd lie in bed at night plotting the deaths of his friends. He even planned how to do it so no one would ever know the culprit. In his shame, Bill blamed his classmates for who he was becoming. His inability to resolve what they did against him led to a horrible permission. Bill began to connect many of the issues of his developing sexuality to the embarrassment of that moment. . . . Sin done against us profoundly affects us. Sometimes it can distort life and cause us to make some incredibly unhealthy judgments. (*TrueFaced*, pages 118-119)

Revisit the three sins or offenses you mentioned in question 1. In what ways (if any) did the pain you felt then distort life and cause you to make unhealthy decisions later?

**4.** In the following questions, we'll share the steps of forgiveness (check this order with what you wrote for question 2).

The first step of forgiveness is: **Admit something happened.**

For example, in Bill's developing adolescence he could've determined he was just going to act tough, be macho, and say, "It was nothing. Didn't bother me at all." Fortunately, he admitted the hurt, or forgiveness would never have occurred. We cannot forgive *until* we admit we have been sinned against. This does not mean we should start searching for all the things we haven't acknowledged were done against us. We're talking about the things we *know* have been done against us that we've chosen to deny. These offenses nag at us, and most will surface automatically. This is an invitation to stop hiding the sin that someone else has done against us. To forgive, we must admit what is already true. (*TrueFaced*, page 120)

Revisit the three offenses you mentioned in question 1. Has it been difficult for you to acknowledge that you were sinned against? If so, why?

Check any reasons you have hesitated to acknowledge or recognize that someone has sinned against you.

☐ I didn't realize it . . . it was so long ago I'd forgotten it.

☐ I didn't want to lose control of the relationship.

☐ I was afraid my offender would manipulate me again or make it my fault.

☐ I didn't want to risk being hurt again if my offender wouldn't admit what happened.

☑ I don't think this should still be bothering me; I just want to move on.

☐ Nobody would believe me.

☐ It wasn't technically a "sin" . . . maybe I was just oversensitive.

☐ Other reasons? _____

**5.** Step two is: **Forgive the consequences of the act done against you.**

Often the consequences of the act done against us are worse—sometimes far worse—than the act of sin itself. . . . As we allow ourselves to feel the pain of our responses, we begin to understand the consequences of the sin done to us. This is critical. (*TrueFaced*, pages 121-122)

Bruce tells of the time several leaders lied to him and then lied about him to others. Their false statements, however, were mild compared to the consequences of those lies: Bruce's loss of reputation, friends, finances, and dreams. His forgiveness had to go far beyond the initial dishonesty and betrayal to include the consequences of the sin. To help you process this critical step of forgiveness, answer Yes or No to these questions in relation to the least resolved of the offenses you mentioned earlier.

**Y   N**   Did I experience shame?

**Y   N**   Did I become fearful?

**Y   N**   Did I feel demeaned and devalued?

**Y   N**   Did anger and resentment begin to grow within me?

**Y   N**   Did I feel manipulated?

**Y   N**   Was I shunned?

**Y   N**   Were there relational effects?

**Y   N**   Did I lose my marriage, my children, my friends?

**Y   N**   Did I lose a business or a sum of money?

**Y   N**   Did I lose my position or leadership role?

**Y   N**   Has this sin led to a change in my outlook or attitude toward life?

Other consequence: _____

Other consequence: _____

**6.** Step three is: **Tell God what happened to you.**

Once we have acknowledged what has happened and how it affected us, we must pour out our hearts to God, telling him everything about what happened to us. . . . We can mumble, cry, sigh, get angry, shout, run around the room, howl like a coyote if we need to—but let's not stop short of getting in touch with all the effects and feelings inside us from that person's sin against us. We shouldn't stop until we're sure we've told God everything that happened to us. Everything. (*TrueFaced*, page 122)

When Bill came to the realization of the power of forgiveness, he forgave his friends for taking off his pants in the stairwell and holding him down. It took him much longer to tell God about the feelings of shame and the pain, about the multiple nights of dreaming of their demise, about his anger, about his self-consciousness, about his blaming them for the inability to date girls. But in time he got it all out. We need to do the same. (*TrueFaced*, pages 122-123)

Some of us, like Bill, find it almost as hard to tell God what happened to us as to admit it to ourselves. Check any reasons below that inhibit you from "taking it to the Lord in prayer."

- ☐ He doesn't want to hear it all.
- ☐ No way! This is only for emotionally based people. I don't do that stuff.
- ☐ God will think I'm complaining.
- ☐ I should be past this.
- ☐ Going over this is just wallowing in it.
- ☐ God already knows these things; he doesn't want to hear it again from me.
- ☐ God has bigger things to worry about than this.
- ☐ Other?

**7.** Step four is: **Forgive the offender for *your* benefit.**

Forgiveness has an order—we must initiate the *vertical transaction* with God before we move into the *horizontal transaction* with others. First, before God, we forgive the offenders for what they've done and the consequences it has reaped in our life. This is between God and us, *for our sake*. Then, after we've forgiven our offenders before God, we go to our offender and forgive him or her. We'll call that a *horizontal transaction*. If we don't get this right, if we move toward the person without having been cleansed before God, we risk moving toward our offender in bitterness, resentment, judgment, and a spirit of getting even. If we prematurely attempt reconciliation with the offender, we'll bring the residue of unresolved sin into the equation. (*TrueFaced*, page 123)

Why do you think it is important to forgive the offender before God *prior to* going to the offender to offer forgiveness? Why is forgiving your offender to *your* benefit?

**8.** Step five is: **Forgive the offender—when they repent—for *their* sake.**

There are three primary reasons for forgiving someone who has sinned against us. After reading each passage that follows, identify who benefits from forgiveness, and how they benefit.

| *TrueFaced* Passage | Who Benefits | How He or She Benefits |
|---|---|---|
| Forgiving the person before God releases us of judgment, bitterness, and resentment toward our offender. When we forgive, our heart heals and we are ready to forgive the one who hurt us—person to person—for that person's sake. (*TrueFaced*, page 124) | | |
| To go to another and declare "I forgive you" before that person repents does nothing for the relationship and robs the offender of the opportunity for his or her own life-freeing repentance. God uses repentance to heal sinful hearts. We shouldn't deprive our offender of that gift. Our forgiveness will not free the other person from their offense, nor will it heal our relationship, if it is premature. The one who sinned against us must repent for his or her own sake—to be healed from sin. Upon the other person's repentance, we can forgive. (*TrueFaced*, pages 124-125) | | |
| We forgive our offender with the goal of restoring the relationship, not just resolving the conflict. We desire our offender's repentance, not to hold it over him or her, but so we can continue on in a healthy relationship. Their repentance won't heal our heart—that is what happens when we forgive our offender before God. But their repentance will heal our *relationship*. (*TrueFaced*, page 125) | | |

What if your offender isn't ready or willing to repent? Should you "force" it? Why or why not?

Read Luke 23:24. When Jesus cried out on the cross, "Father, forgive them," was his cry a demonstration of Step four (forgiving his offenders before God for *his* sake)? Or was it a demonstration of Step five (forgiving his offenders face-to-face for *their* sake)? Explain.

**9.** Step six is: **Distinguish between forgiving and trusting your offender.**

Forgiveness does not mean we have to trust the other person yet. . . . Forgiving the person and trusting the person again are always separate issues. Even if we have forgiven our offender—even if our offender has repented and asked our forgiveness—we will still, in the future, have to deal with the issue of mutual trust. Trustworthiness must be evaluated. Our expectations should be realistic because while trust is easily broken, it is recovered very slowly, and sometimes not at all. Forgiveness carries the hope of renewed trust in the offender, but it does not mandate or guarantee it. (*TrueFaced*, page 126)

Is there someone in your life whom you just don't trust? Why not? Is your mistrust connected to a past offense? Have you forgiven them? Why? Why not? On the basis of your trusting God through forgiveness, what do you need to do to extend trust? What do you believe they should do to earn your trust?

**10.** The final step is: **Seek reconciliation, not just conflict resolution.**

In your opinion, what is the difference between resolving a conflict and restoring a relationship? What words would you begin with if you want to:

- resolve a conflict with someone? ___*beat it!*_____
- restore a relationship with someone? _____

Meditate on these words of Jesus about forgiveness:

> If a fellow believer hurts you [sins against you — NIV], go and tell him — work it out between the two of you. If he listens, you've made a friend [you have won your brother over — NIV]. If he won't listen, take one or two others along so that the presence of witnesses will keep things honest, and try again. If he still won't listen, tell the church. If he won't listen to the church, you'll have to start over from scratch, confront him with the need for repentance, and offer again God's forgiving love. (Matthew 18:15-17, MSG)

According to Jesus, what is the primary purpose of pursuing the issue between you? Do you believe you could do this if you had not first forgiven him or her before God for your own sake?

Meditate on these words of Paul about forgiveness and reconciliation.

> All this comes from the God who settled the relationship between us and him, and then called us to settle our relationships with each other. God put the world square with himself through the Messiah, giving the world a fresh start by offering forgiveness of sins. God has given us the task of telling

everyone what he is doing. We're Christ's representative.
God uses us to persuade men and women to drop their differ
ences and enter into God's work of making things righ
between them. We're speaking for Christ himself nov
Become friends with God; he's already a friend with you
How? you say. In Christ. God put the wrong on him wh
never did anything wrong, so we could be put right with Goc
(2 Corinthians 5:18-21, MSC

Circle any phrase in the preceding passage that describes reconciliation.
According to these verses, from God's perspective, how important is it for
us to be reconciled to him? How important is it to God that we become
reconciled to one another? What is the connection between the two recon-
ciliations? Explain.

# Experiencing TrueFaced Together

## Before you begin:

**1.** Get together with your group. If you are a part of a large group (such as a church school class), your teacher or leader will facilitate the experience. If you're doing this in a small-group setting, anyone can lead the group by following the directions in this section.

**2.** Consider the following guidelines for making the most of your group experience:

- When you are directed to form a small group for an activity, select people you know at least a little. If you are placed in a pair or trio with people you don't know, take a couple minutes to introduce yourselves. This will give you a good starting place for today's experiential activity.
- Follow the directions carefully, particularly as they relate to discussion in your small group. These directions have been designed to provide safe boundaries so you can share appropriately with others.
- The skills, techniques, and truths you discover during this experience are applicable in many other areas of life. Practice what you learn outside of small-group time.
- Above all, don't be anxious about the experiential activities in this guide. They aren't scary, "stand up in front of the group and share your life" experiences. Each Experiencing TrueFaced Together activity has been field-tested and is designed to ease you into participation. That's not to say what you learn will be fluffy, surface-level stuff. The experiences can be life-changing. We'll lead you into the deeper stuff. But come prepared to invest yourself in the experience. It will be worth it.

## For the Group Leader

If you are the designated leader for this TrueFaced Experience, please follow these guidelines to ensure a positive experience for all participants.

**1.** Make sure everyone has the necessary materials before the session. Each person should have a copy of *TrueFaced* and a copy of the *TrueFaced Experience Guide*. You'll also need a copy of the *TrueFaced Experience DVD* set for your group. This session uses DVD #2.

**2.** Review the DVD contents for each session and know right where to go to play them. Test your DVD player setup to avoid technical glitches.

**3.** You are a facilitator for this, not a teacher. Follow the instructions closely and fight any temptation to expand on the material provided. This is a place for experiential learning, *not* lecture.

**4.** Don't worry if some questions are left unanswered. Unanswered questions are part of the discovery process.

**5.** Close the session with prayer, and then remind participants of their homework assignments for the coming session.

# Healing

## Welcome

Take a moment to greet one another. If you traditionally enjoy snacks with your group, have at 'em. Use the opening moments as people congregate for a brief time of fellowship.

## Video Introduction

Gather in front of the TV/monitor and watch the video introduction to this session. It's called "Week 7: Healing/Forgiveness" in your DVD menu.

## Introducing the Experience

Today we're going to apply TrueFaced principles in an activity we call "Forgiving." This experience helps us experience healing like few gifts in life. One thing is true of every one of us—we have all been hurt. Sometimes we're hurt by people who sin against us. Sometimes we're hurt even when people don't sin against us. In either case, healing comes through experiencing the most mysterious gift in The Room of Grace—forgiveness.

## For an Enjoyable Experience

In order to make this experience excellent and beneficial to all, consider the following guidelines for your small- and large-group time:

- Bring a mindset that says, "I am for the other person's best."
- Allow other group members to answer their questions. Do not interrupt.
- Allow other group members to "keep" their answers. Do not correct.
- Allow other group members to share their answers. Do not counsel. Listening to others talk about their experiences is a wonderful affirmation for them.
- Allow other group members to experience safety. Do not discuss their answers outside your group, unless they give you permission to do so.

## About the DVD

We highly recommend you use the DVD for your TrueFaced Experience as it adds a significant dimension to the study. John Lynch is your DVD host and offers lots of good thoughts and compelling real-life stories that can help you in your journey. However, if you don't have access to the DVD, you can alternately have someone read aloud John's abbreviated introduction that follows.

**John Lynch:** Forgiveness can seem like an impossible thing to do. We need a way home. We've been told to get over the sin done to us, but we can't find our way out of the shadows. We can't seem to let go of our hurt.

I got hurt by a friend . . . a good friend. The violation at the time seemed so enormous that I refused to resolve it. I held onto it with a self-vindicating chokehold of self-righteous judgment. That morphed into bitterness. Bitterness began to release incredible shame and blame in me. Shame colored everything I did.

On the other hand, I was obsessed with judging, convicting, and passing sentence upon my violator. I lost all objectivity. I also had a hard time receiving love. *I couldn't trust the love friends were offering.* I nearly moved my family during this time. I was willing to trade it all to escape the pain and preoccupation with myself. If not for God's stubborn refusal, I would have chucked it all.

Forgiveness breaks down walls, frees hearts, mends countries, restores families. It can turn hatred into tenderness and the desire to destroy into a passion to protect. When we forgive, hearts are woven together in love. This powerful gift has this purpose: to protect us from the insidious harm that has come from sin done against us.

During our exercise today, we'll explore how far we have come, or where we may presently be on that journey of forgiveness. It is tricky work, discerning our hearts. Let those in this group, who you've been growing to depend upon, help you walk through an honest evaluation of how you're handling forgiveness. It's a gift that will keep giving for a lifetime.

## The "Forgiving" Experience

**1.** Begin by forming a small group with one or two partners. Groups of three work best. This experience should take approximately 30 minutes.

**2.** In your small group, have each person choose one of the questions in the "Forgiving Questions" box. Each small group member may answer any question—you don't have to all answer the same question although it's certainly okay if you do.

**3.** Take turns in your group sharing your answer to the question you've chosen. As others in your small group are talking, listen intently. Ask yourself "What am I learning?" not "What can I teach the others?" Consider what clarifying questions you might ask once a group member is done talking. Clarifying questions include: "What did you mean by . . . ," "How did that affect you . . . ," or "Did you say . . . " questions but not "Why" questions. You might want to jot these down in the "Notes" space.

**4.** After answering your question, have the rest of the group members each ask one clarifying question.

**5.** Pray for each group member after all clarifying questions have been answered. Then if you still have time, have each group member choose another question to answer and follow the same instructions.

## orgiving Questions

**1.** Describe a time when admitting something was done to you was critical to your healing.

**2.** What makes it difficult to admit something was done to you?

**3.** Describe ways forgiveness has healed you from sin done against you.

**4.** Why do you think it's crucial to forgive others for the consequences of their actions against us?

**5.** You can invite others in your group to suggest a new question for you to answer. This can be risky, but very rewarding. You choose whether to answer it or one of the questions provided.

**Notes:**

## Processing the "Forgiving" Experience

Form one large group and discuss the following question for no more than three minutes: *What did you just experience?* Allow time for everyone who so desires to respond. Stay focused on the processing question and use the guidelines outlined previously to facilitate a healthy discussion.

## Closing Video and Prayer

After exploring the processing question together, play the video segment called "Week 7: Healing/Forgiveness Recap" on your DVD menu. Following this, close in prayer and review the homework for next week's session.

## Before the Next Session

Read chapter 7, "Maturing into God's Dreams for You," in your *TrueFaced* book. Then complete the "Experiencing TrueFaced on Your Own" section for Week Eight in this Experience Guide (go to page 143). Pray throughout the week that your discoveries will positively impact all aspects of your everyday life.

## About the DVD

We highly recommend you use the DVD for your TrueFaced Experience as it adds a significant dimension to the study. However, if you don't have access to this DVD, you can alternately have someone read aloud the summary that follows.

**John Lynch:** This stuff about forgiving for my sake, so that I can forgive for another's sake, may initially make as much sense as: 2 + 2 = magnesium! Don't forget this truth: God *knows*. And he loves you, accepts you, and delights in you. He has seen your pain and that's why he's giving you this gift. This is one of the last hurdles to cross in our journey. And it may be your most important. Follow the steps, believe God's protection, trust his plan. Today, before you go to bed, pray this thought to God: "Lord, would you make me ready to let go?" And if you mean it, he will.

# Introducing the Tool

If you want to go deeper with your TrueFaced experience, take time in the coming week to complete the "Forgiving Tool" on your own. This tool gives you an opportunity to actually *act* on the truths in *TrueFaced*. Character is formed as we *act on truth* that touches our hearts. Acting is how we know we are *trusting* the truth. After you have completed your part of the exercise, share it with one or two trusted friends. (It's important that your friends read the corresponding chapter in *TrueFaced* so they can fully understand the process you are experiencing. Share your copy of *TrueFaced* or encourage them to buy a copy for themselves.)

## Forgiving Tool

**1.** Describe the price you pay (and may be paying today) for not receiving God's grace gift of forgiveness. Explain this price in one or more of the following areas:

- Relational (loss of intimacy with God and others, loss of influence, loss of opportunities)
- Spiritual/Emotional (spiritual dryness, loss of focus, pain, lack of healing, loss of creativity, heaviness, sense of imprisonment)
- Physical (sleep loss, energy loss, illness)
- Circumstantial (financial, job or asset loss)

**2.** Describe the price you believe you would have to pay for forgiving. Explain this price in one or more of the following ways:

- Giving up control in a relationship
- Losing reputation
- Trusting God and others instead of yourself
- Acknowledging you were wrong
- Letting go of your hurt

**3.** Which "prices" do you want to continue paying, those from question 1 or question 2? (If you choose question 2, don't attempt to "will yourself" into forgiveness. Forgiveness is a gift from God. Healing forgiveness is impossible without his grace, which in turn is made possible by Jesus' sacrifice. When you *trust* this grace gift, you *receive* it. You align with what he wants you to be and do. Healing means that you are moving into The Room of Grace where your relationships can be restored. So right now, trust God's assessment of what you should believe and enjoy the *rest* and *healing* that comes with this gift.)

**4.** As you receive this gift, *follow God into the action* for which you are trusting him. If you do not know what he is asking you to do, ask your trusted friends if they have thoughts or counsel for you.

# Week Eight: Dreams

# Experiencing TrueFaced on Your Own

## Before you begin:

**1.** Read chapter 7, "Maturing into God's Dreams for You" in your *TrueFaced* book. Take time to soak up all the stories and thoughts. This will be the basis for answering the following questions. You may want to review the "Did You Discover?" questions at the end of the chapter as well. To dig even further into the background for this chapter, look up the related Scripture passages referenced in the back of the *TrueFaced* book in the "Notes" section.

**2.** Get out a pen or pencil and respond to the questions that follow. Keep in mind this is your personal workbook for examining the truths in *TrueFaced*. It's okay to spill the truth onto these pages: they are "for your eyes only." Let this become a journal of your exploration of what it means to be TrueFaced.

## Dreams

**1.** God dreams that you would discover your destiny and walk into the reasons he placed you on this earth. God has a ticket of destiny with your name written on it—no matter how old, how broken, how tired, or how frightened you are. No matter how many times you may have failed, God dearly longs for the day when he gets to hand you that ticket, smile, and whisper into your ear, "You have no idea how long I've waited to hand this to you. Have a blast! I've already seen what you get to do. It's better than you could have dreamed. Now hurry up and get on that train. A whole lot of folk are waiting for you to walk into your destiny and into their lives." (*TrueFaced*, page 13)

What is the difference between your dreams and your destiny? How are they related?

When you were growing up, what dreams did you have for your future? What did you dream you would do, or have, or be?

As you look back, which parts of those childhood dreams of yours do you believe were actually whispers of God's dreams for you? Explain.

**2.** People in The Room of Good Intentions never get released into the dreams God has for them. Everyone here is trying to change into someone else to appease God. We hide, position, strive, perfect our self-effort, and polish our image. We often interpret our ability to compete well against each other as a sign of our godliness and success. We look very impressive—we have learned to package our techniques well—but our self-effort keeps us self-centered and immature.

> As we said in chapter 2, whenever we are trapped in shame or blame or anger, for any period of time, we stop maturing. This is what happens when we lodge in The Room of Good Intentions. We may become competent and skilled. We may achieve position and significant-looking roles. We do stuff—maybe even impressive stuff. But, because we are constantly pursuing power and authority, and manipulating to gain control, God can never release us into our future. Our relational sadness, our inability to be loved, our festering wounds and broken relationships freeze us in immaturity. Without humility, we continue to miss the train that takes us into God's intention for our destiny. (*TrueFaced*, pages 133-134)

What are things that go on in The Room of Good Intentions that prevent us from maturing? (Underline them in the excerpt above.) Which one of these things grieves you the most—in yourself or in others?

**3.** Imagine the journey of *Maturing into Your Destiny* as climbing stairs (see next page).

\_\_\_\_\_ Released into Destiny

\_\_\_\_\_ Maturing

\_\_\_\_\_ Healing

\_\_\_\_\_ Granting Forgiveness

\_\_\_\_\_ Experiencing Repentance

\_\_\_\_\_ Receiving Love

\_\_\_\_\_ God Standing with Me to Resolve My Sin

\_\_\_\_\_ Living in the Room of Grace

\_\_\_\_\_ Living Out of Who God Says I Am

\_\_\_\_\_ Trusting God

Draw yourself on the step you believe you are standing on today.

Draw a footprint on the next step you believe God wants you to take. Explain.

**4.** We who dwell in The Room of Grace have come to believe who God says we are. We're not trying to change into another person. God has made us exactly who he wants us to be, and we have come to believe it. Any change that takes place in us comes from maturing into the person we already are—much like a caterpillar matures into a butterfly. (*TrueFaced*, page 135)

How does our choice of "rooms" influence our destiny?

How does our choice of "rooms" influence our maturity?

**5.** The mature in this room have also learned how to live with a community of people who trust God and others with what is true about them. We—and the others in this community—have taken off our masks and are learning to walk in the resplendent freedom and purposes of God. But we remember the pain of letting go of our masks; we still carry the scars from where the glue tore our skin. We are not free from visible problems and issues just because we no longer hide them. Our issues are there for everyone to see. Sometimes the mature homeowners in The Room of Grace appear to have more issues than the prize citizens of The Room of Good Intentions. We depend upon God and his power and resources. We are free to trust him for repentance. We are free to trust him so we can forgive others and be forgiven. . . . But such maturity does not happen overnight. God uses many others for our benefit in this process. Some are teachers, counselors, friends, pastors, spouses, siblings, children, mentors, disciplers, spiritual guides, and spiritual directors. (*TrueFaced*, pages 135-136)

Think of two people who have impacted your personal maturing by providing a safe, grace-filled relationship where you can reveal what is true about you. Describe those two people and your situation.

Grace-Giver #1:

Grace-Giver #2:

**6.** Maturity in The Room of Grace occurs in three general phases. Of course, these phases overlap with each other, and we often jump back and forth in our development.

- Phase One: Healing the Needy Christian
- Phase Two: Maturing the Healing Christian
- Phase Three: Releasing the Maturing Christian
  (*TrueFaced*, pages 136-138)

Where are you in these phases? Explain.

**7.** One of the greatest gifts we can offer another person is a safe place to fail. In this room, teachers and mentors help youthful followers of Christ to learn the priority of not hiding. This is such a place—a room where they can disclose what is really true about the sin in them and the sin that has been done against them. Such a gift at this phase in a believer's life is profound and freeing. (*TrueFaced*, page 137)

Why do you think we need to be free to fail? Briefly describe a failure in your life. How did you and others respond to your failure?

**8.** Reread the material on Phase Three (*TrueFaced*, pages 138-139). From this passage, summarize the attributes of a Maturing Christian's inner life, as well as attributes of his or her relationships with and influence upon others.

| Maturing Christian's Inner Life | Maturing Christian's Relational Life/Influence |
|---|---|
| | |

**9.** What do the following Scriptures tell you about God's dreams for his children? What do they also say about our part in seeing these dreams fulfilled?

| Verse | God's Dreams for His Children | The Part We Play |
|---|---|---|
| Jeremiah 29:11-13 | | |
| Ephesians 2:8-10 | | |
| 1 Peter 5:5-6 | | |

**10.** The same God who dreamt dreams of Joseph and Esther and the rest, continues to dream dreams and design destinies for every single one of his children. Think of some historical and contemporary Christians, or anyone not mentioned in the Bible, whom you believe were released into their God-given destinies—people whose destiny and influence you admire. For each one, give name, destiny, and primary field of influence.

| Person | Destiny | Field of Influence |
|---|---|---|
| Mother Teresa | To bring comfort, dignity, and hospice care | To the poor and dying in Calcutta and beyond |
| Keith Green | To touch through prophetic music | The "lukewarm" parts of Christ's Church |
|  |  |  |
|  |  |  |
|  |  |  |
|  |  |  |

**11.** Listen, and hear God speak to you through his Word below. End this study in a time of worship and praise to your one true Audience—your Father—for his gracious invitation to live TrueFaced before him and the world.

> I am GOD. I have called you to live right and well. I have taken responsibility for you, kept you safe. I have set you among my people to bind them to me, and provided you as a lighthouse to the nations. . . . Through him we received both the generous gift of his life and the urgent task of passing it on to others who receive it by entering into obedient trust in Jesus. You are who you are through this gift and call of Jesus Christ! . . . There has never been the slightest doubt in my mind that the God who started this great work in you would keep at it and bring it to a flourishing finish on the very day Christ Jesus appears.
> (Isaiah 42:6, Romans 1:5-6, and Philippians 1:6, MSG.

# Experiencing TrueFaced Together

## Before you begin:

**1.** Get together with your group. If you are a part of a large group (such as a church school class), your teacher or leader will facilitate the experience. If you're doing this in a small-group setting, anyone can lead the group by following the directions in this section.

**2.** Consider the following guidelines for making the most of your group experience:

- When you are directed to form a small group for an activity, select people you know at least a little. If you are placed in a pair or trio with people you don't know, take a couple minutes to introduce yourselves. This will give you a good starting place for today's experiential activity.
- Follow the directions carefully, particularly as they relate to discussion in your small group. These directions have been designed to provide safe boundaries so you can share appropriately with others.
- The skills, techniques, and truths you discover during this experience are applicable in many other areas of life. Practice what you learn outside of small-group time.
- Above all, don't be anxious about the experiential activities in this guide. They aren't scary, "stand up in front of the group and share your life" experiences. Each Experiencing TrueFaced Together activity has been field-tested and is designed to ease you into participation. That's not to say what you learn will be fluffy, surface-level stuff. The experiences can be life-changing. We'll lead you into the deeper stuff. But come prepared to invest yourself in the experience. It will be worth it.

## For the Group Leader

If you are the designated leader for this TrueFaced Experience, please follow these guidelines to ensure a positive experience for all participants.

**1.** Make sure everyone has the necessary materials before the session. Each person should have a copy of *TrueFaced* and a copy of the *TrueFaced Experience Guide*. You'll also need a copy of the *TrueFaced Experience DVD* set for your group. This session uses DVD #2.

**2.** Review the DVD contents for each session and know right where to go to play them. Test your DVD player setup to avoid technical glitches.

**3.** You are a facilitator for this, not a teacher. Follow the instructions closely and fight any temptation to expand on the material provided. This is a place for experiential learning, *not* lecture.

**4.** Don't worry if some questions are left unanswered. Unanswered questions are part of the discovery process.

**5.** Close the session with prayer, and then remind participants of their homework assignments for the coming session.

# Dreams

## Welcome

Take a moment to greet one another. If you traditionally enjoy snacks with your group, have at 'em. Use the opening moments as people congregate for a brief time of fellowship.

## Video Introduction

Gather in front of the TV/monitor and watch the video introduction to this session. It's called "Week 8: Dreams/Influence" in your DVD menu.

## Introducing the Experience

Today we're going to apply TrueFaced principles in an activity we call "Influencing." This experience helps us stop at the summit and look back at the amazing vistas God has shown us during our *TrueFaced* journey.

## For an Enjoyable Experience

In order to make this experience excellent and beneficial to all, consider the following guidelines for your small- and large-group time:

- Bring a mindset that says, "I am for the other person's best."
- Allow other group members to answer their questions. Do not interrupt.
- Allow other group members to share their answers. Do not counsel. Listening to others talk about their experiences is a wonderful affirmation for them.

## The "Influencing" Experience

**1.** Begin by forming a small group with one or two partners. Groups of three work best. This experience should take approximately 20 minutes.

**2.** On your own, reflect on the questions in the "Influencing Questions" box. Take about five minutes to do this.

## About the DVD

We highly recommend you use the DVD for your TrueFaced Experience as it adds a significant dimension to the study. John Lynch is your DVD host and offers lots of good thoughts and compelling real-life stories that can help you in your journey. However, if you don't have access to the DVD, you can alternately have someone read aloud John's abbreviated introduction that follows.

**John Lynch:** While healing is precious almost beyond telling, it isn't nearly enough. Healing is just part of the vehicle driving us to God's goal—our destiny, the dreams he has shaped in the deepest part of our being. No matter how many times you may have failed, God dearly longs for the day when he gets to hand you that incredible ticket with your name on it.

My friend Bob never had the words to describe what he was longing for. Though he is an accomplished graphic artist, a brilliant writer and playwright, a masterful director, an excellent actor, songwriter, and performer, most of his Christian life Bob has been deeply troubled with significant and severe issues of unresolved relational sin. Twelve years ago, Bob discovered and chose to enter The Room of Grace. During the years since, he has fallen back into the darkness of hidden duplicity more than once. But The Room of Grace is not a place where we do not sin—it is a place where we are protected by those who love us.

Today, Bob understands that he is a man loved by God. Now he lives in a humble realization that in spite of what is true about him, he does not have to be a victim of his own sometimes-sinful choices. He is, by faith, who God says he is even on his worst day.

[Bob sings his original song, *Sometimes by Faith*. See Lyrics in *TrueFaced* pages 143-144]

**3.** Then take turns in your group sharing your answer to the questions. As others in your small group are talking, listen intently.

**4.** After everyone has shared, pause and thank God for his gifts.

## Influencing Questions

**1.** Which part of the journey has had the most life-changing impression on you? Explain.

- Hope/Truth-Telling
- Authenticity/Unmasking
- Identity/Connecting
- Safety/Accepting Others
- Love/Granting Permission
- Freedom/Repenting
- Healing/Forgiving
- Dreams/Influencing

**2.** How will this part of the journey change the way you will influence others in the future? (Influencing others is central to the dreams God has for you.)

Notes:

## Processing the "Influencing" Experience

Form one large group and discuss the following question for no more than ten minutes: *What did you just experience?* Allow time for everyone who so desires to respond. Stay focused on the processing question and use the guidelines outlined previously to facilitate a healthy discussion.

## Closing Video and Prayer

After exploring the processing question together, play the video segment called "Week 8: Dreams/Influence Recap" for John's summary of this eight-week experience. Thank God for allowing you to experience what it means to live in The Room of Grace — and ask him to reveal his dreams and destiny for you as you live out these truths.

# Introducing the Tool

If you want to go deeper with your TrueFaced experience, take time in the coming week to complete the "Influencing Tool" on your own. This tool gives you an opportunity to actually *act* on the truths in *TrueFaced*. Character is formed as we *act on truth* that touches our hearts. Acting is how we know we are *trusting* the truth. After you have completed your part of the exercise, share it with one or two trusted friends. (It's important that your friends read the corresponding chapter in *TrueFaced* so they can fully understand the process you are experiencing. Share your copy of *TrueFaced* or encourage them to buy a copy for themselves.)

## Influencing Tool

God's dreams for us are real. But they are also mysterious, in that they are *his* dreams for us, not ours. At the same time, God's dreams for us are *not* mysterious in that they will *always* involve serving God by serving and influencing others. God continues to mature us through serving others.

**1.** Dreams are about *asking*. What should you be asking about God's dreams for you? Who should you be asking? (Ask at least two people who are close to you what they believe may be in your future based on your interests, background, strengths, limitations, opportunities, talents, gifts, and training.)

**2.** Dreams are about *waiting*. In what areas or ways is God asking you to wait? (Is God asking you to not pursue a particular job or career at this time? Is he asking you to relax about a specific relational tension? Is he asking you to help someone else succeed in a role you really wanted for yourself? Ask one or two friends to evaluate your motive in waiting. Why are you waiting?)

**3.** Dreams are about *preparing*. In what ways is God asking you to prepare? (This could be studying God's dreams for those in Scripture; training to develop your talents or gifts in some way; visiting a country foreign to you; writing your stories for others to read and learn from; finding a mentor; developing key relationships with those who can stand with you; and so forth.)

**4.** Dreams are about *receiving*. How does humility allow you to receive your dream? (If you want to revisit the relationship between humility and destiny, pick up a copy of *Beyond Your Best* or *The Ascent of a Leader* from Leadership Catalyst).

**5.** Share your written answers with your trusted friends. Place these answers where you will see them often, perhaps in a journal, in your personal planner, or in your Bible. These answers will become reminders of a valuable journey and guideposts to still more adventures in discovering the dreams God has wisely and lovingly planned for you.

# RESOURCES FOR INDIVIDUALS AND SMALL GROUPS FROM LEADERSHIP CATALYST

In addition to this *TrueFaced Experience Guide*, Leadership Catalyst offers a variety of spiritual formation resources for individuals and groups.

If you have not yet completed the eight-module *Beyond Your Best Experience Guide*, we encourage you to make it your next journey.

Pick up one of the *Beyond Your Best* or *TrueFaced* card decks, which include insights for each week. Check out our Affirmation Tools and other tools for teams, marriages, and families.

These resources can be ordered online at leadershipcatalyst.org or by calling 888-249-0700.

# RESOURCES FOR ORGANIZATIONS FROM LEADERSHIP CATALYST

One word has the power to catalyze greatness in an individual, an organization, or a nation: *Trust*. Surveys show that trust is the #1 requirement for success in life and leadership. But for many, trust has been hard to come by or misplaced. There is a painful Trust Gap . . . and it appears to be widening in many arenas of business, education, government, church, and even family life.

The *mission* of Leadership Catalyst is to build and restore *trust* in leaders and those they influence. Established in 1995, Leadership Catalyst is recognized as an international resource for helping leaders learn how to develop trust and authentic environments of increased character, vision, and productivity.

Leadership Catalyst has designed a groundbreaking process to help leaders and their teams bridge the Trust Gap and reshape their cultures. Delivery of the learning process is implemented through your organization's Master Coaches, who are trained in Catalyst Clinics.

For additional information on Leadership Catalyst and our latest resource catalog, please contact us directly:

Leadership Catalyst, Inc.
1600 E Northern Ave, Suite 280
Phoenix, AZ 85020
Voice 602-249-7000
Voice 888-249-0700 (Toll-free in North America)
Fax 602-249-0611
Email: *info@leadershipcatalyst.org*
Website: www.leadershipcatalyst.org